What others are saying about
Read the Room for Real:

"David Campt and Matthew Freeman are well known as the foremost experts on the use of audience response systems to enhance meeting quality and public engagement. In this book, they have collected and shared numerous critical insights from their vast experiences over the years, and clearly make the case for the value audience polling can add to a wide variety of contexts. Their "SPEIK" model clearly represents the state of the art, and has set a new standard that will push the field to new heights."

> Martín Carcasson
> Founder and Director
> Colorado State University Center for Public Deliberation

"We have witnessed firsthand how the appropriate use of technology can help activate and engage citizens in large public gatherings. This book is a practical tool for getting the most out of your meetings, and for using essential data gathered to better guide the process."

> Kristin Williams
> Director of Community Initiatives
> The Sherwood Foundation

"The authors are both experienced designers, organizers, and facilitators of all kinds of public engagement, and so the book is a trove of practical guidance for using speed polling in a variety of situations. Campt and Freeman also delve into some of the larger, thornier questions about the limits and potential of speed polling, and engagement itself; they do this in a way that is both insightful and pragmatic. *Read the Room for Real* is an essential guide for engagement practitioners and scholars alike."

> Matt Leighninger
> Executive Director
> Deliberative Democracy Consortium

"Campt and Freeman's book provides clear, concise, concrete, and compelling techniques to achieving the art and science of facilitated dialogue. Beyond being merely instructive (which it certainly is), this book presents the imperative for why inclusivity matters—and how to achieve this difficult, but essential, goal."

Emily M. Janke, Ph.D.
Associate Professor, Peace and Conflict Studies
Director, Institute for Community and Economic Engagement (ICEE)
University of North Carolina Greensboro

"If you have ever thought about using audience polling to augment your meetings, you need to get this book! The authors have a well-deserved national reputation for creating great group experiences with clickers, and in this book they clearly explain how to create the magic that can happen through facilitating with the technology. The book goes beyond how to make meetings more engaging, but also addresses some benefits of the technology that I had not really considered. I highly recommend *Read the Room for Real* for anyone in the facilitation business who wants to know more about how to take their meetings to the next level of effectiveness."

Sandy Heierbacher
Director
National Coalition for Dialogue and Deliberation

"This riveting book will help anyone planning any type of meeting; from energizing staff meetings, to making decisions in schools or communities, to running a family reunion, a business or even a country."

Lisa Schirch
Director
Human Security, Alliance for Peacebuilding
Eastern Mennonite University

Read the Room
for Real

Other Books by David Campt

The Little Book of Dialogue for Difficult Subjects

Read the Room
for Real
How a Simple Technology Creates Better Meetings

DAVID W. CAMPT

WITH MATTHEW FREEMAN

Foreword by
Carolyn Lukensmeyer
National Center for Civil Discourse

I AM Publications

I AM Publications books may be purchased for educational, business, or sales promotional use. Special discounts are available on quantity purchases by corporations, associations, and others.
For details, contact the publisher at the following address.

For information, please call or write:

I AM Publications
105 Springfield Street
Chicopee, MA 01013.
Telephone: (617) 564-1060
Fax: (617) 831-1629
Or visit www.iampubs.com

Printed in the United States of America

Second Edition, 2015

ISBN 978-1-943-38200-2

Book Design and Editing:
Hazel Edwards
hazelredwards@gmail.com

DEDICATION

To those who think that all of us are smarter than any of us

CONTENTS

ACKNOWLEDGMENTS

Writing any book is an endeavor that I could not do without assistance. I am grateful to so many people for all the help they provided, but space only allows me to mention a small number.

To Carolyn Lukensmeyer, Steve Brigham, polling fanatic Mike Smith and all the employees and associates at AmericaSpeaks: Thanks for first exposing me to audience polling and the magic that emerges when a meeting design is based on a deep appreciation for each attendee's experience and contribution.

To Angela Oh and Chris and Julia Sullivan: Thank you for responding so generously to my request that you read my early draft—and for doing so even though I had not been in touch for a while. I am so glad this project reconnected us.

Shout outs to Junette Pinkney, McCrae Parker, and Lisa Thompson for keeping my physical and psychological houses in order. Each of you has done the right amount of chastising, cajoling, laying on of spiritual hands and old fashioned encouragement, and saying, "C'mon man!" at the appropriate times.

Thanks to the "bar/offices" that were willing to provide a weird-looking guy in a corner table virtually unlimited refills on coffee and did so with incredible hospitality. If readers are ever in Madison, North Carolina, have the stromboli at the Blue Naples; likewise, in Eden, North Carolina, go to the Red River Grill and have any of the 55 flavors of wings, as well as the oatmeal at the Sirloin House.

To Dan Tuden, Mike Barney, and Theo Brown: Your willingness to provide feedback while calming my insecurities and tangibly improving the document was indispensable. Once again, each of you has shown what it means to be a brother from another mother.

To my sister from another mister Paulina Borsook: Despite my always having talked about the high cost of free services, your pro bono editing services have a value beyond measure. I just hope that when I pay it forward it has half the impact that your help has had.

To Dr. Hazel Edwards who stepped in to provide content editing, copy corrections, and graphic design expertise: you have been critical in taking a fine preview edition to a great new level. My cup of gratitude runneth over for your dedication, professionalism, and plain ole' talent.

To my brilliant, occasional partner Kevin Williams: You have been an invaluable inspiration when it comes to the importance of translating deep-seated intentions into effective actions. This book would not have happened without your unique methods of showing me the way forward.

To my lovely wife Vietta Johnson and daughter Arnai: Our family has provided many critical lessons for me about the importance of dedication, courage, focus, and daily discipline. May these lessons stick with me as we stick to each other.

To Ngozi Robinson, principal of I Am Publications: Thanks for maintaining your belief in me through the trials and vicissitudes. I love our strange and glorious partnership—may it never change.

To my co-author Matthew Freeman: I sometimes think you are the only person who understands one of my deepest passions. Our fellowship in the keypad ministry has been more important than you could know.

And of course, my most enduring gratitude goes to James and Geraldine Campt. Without you, I would not have my deep commitment to creating dialogue that reaches people's souls and lifts their spirits. The lessons you have taught me have made me who I am in countless ways.

FOREWORD

In today's world we conduct the vast majority of our communication online, which makes it even more important that the time we spend face-to-face in meetings be engaging and productive. And yet far too often we find ourselves complaining about how a poorly run meeting has wasted our time.

David and Matthew are passionate about the power and beauty of effective meetings and have written a book that not only inspires others to create better meetings but gives them the know-how to actually do it.

The heart of the book revolves around the value of using handheld polling devices that enable you to "read the room for real." The power of this simple technology rests in its capacity to enable every individual in the room to vote and then allows the person running the meeting to very quickly calculate and share the collective outcomes of that vote. You can use it to show the demographics of who is in the room, the level of existing knowledge or the range of viewpoints about a key issue, the collective priorities of all present for action, the shared evaluation and level of confidence in what is happening, all in real time in the room. In other words you can instantly engage the people present in understanding and owning significant data about themselves: who they are, what they think, what they want to do, how committed they are, how much fun they are having, or whatever data is relevant to the purposes and desired outcomes of the meeting.

Like any other technology keypads can be used well or poorly. The most significant contribution of this book is that it teaches you specifically how to use the technology effectively. Through the use of very interesting case examples, by breaking down each step of the design and phases of an effective meeting and clarifying how the keypads work in a variety of kinds of meetings, the authors have actively engaged the reader in a seminar on effective use. It is almost as if they are in the same room with you anticipating your next question.

For most of us organizing and participating in meetings on a regular basis, time is our most precious resource. David and Matthew have given us a great gift in the understanding of how to design meetings utilizing an accessible and simple technology that both saves time and makes the time spent more meaningful, engaging and productive. Let's help them spread the word!

> Carolyn Lukensmeyer
> Washington, DC
> October, 2014

Carolyn J. Lukensmeyer, Ph.D. is the Executive Director of the National Institute for Civil Discourse which works with elected officials, media, and the public to reduce incivility and political dysfunction. Previously she founded and was the President of AmericaSpeaks, which created the 21st Century Town Meeting to bring citizens to the table to influence the decisions that impact their lives. Keypad polling devices were one of the technologies AmericaSpeaks used to support the public reaching collective decisions on city budgets, regional plans, rebuilding lower Manhattan after 9/11, priorities for recovery in New Orleans after hurricanes Katrina and Rita, healthcare reform in California, and a myriad of other issues. She also served as the first woman Chief of Staff in the State of Ohio. Prior to that she led her own management consulting firm where she designed and facilitated meetings in every sector nationally and internationally.

PREFACE

David's facilitation career began in the late 1980s, when he was a graduate student at the University of California, Berkeley. There, he co-taught courses on race relations and created dialogues about cultural competence within local social service agencies. After completing his doctorate in city planning, he served as Senior Policy Advisor at the White House as part of the Presidential Initiative on Race. One of his responsibilities was the design of televised public dialogues for President Clinton, and another was the construction of multi-state dialogue campaigns.

After leaving the White House, David worked as an organizational consultant. He served a wide variety of clients, including Fortune 500 companies, international peace organizations, and various agencies within federal, state, and local government. He did not become familiar with techniques for using instantaneous polling until 1999, when he became involved with the sadly now defunct AmericaSpeaks. The organization had pioneered a process for convening deliberations that would involve anywhere from dozens to thousands of people. David was particularly intrigued by the impact of instant audience polling on group dynamics. Even though AmericaSpeaks integrated instant polling into its highly polished dialogic process, it was clear to David that audience polling could be, on its own, a powerful and affordable meeting innovation.

Matthew had been facilitating since his college days at William and Mary, when he was a resident assistant tasked with facilitating conversations among freshman about what dorm rules they wanted to live by. Since then, he has loved the challenge of helping keep conversations about controversial topics productive and fruitful.

After getting his Masters at the University of British Columbia, Matthew returned to his hometown of Richmond, Virginia, and began working with a variety of non-profits who used dialogue facilitation as a tool to overcome the city's toxic racial history.

In 2006, Matthew became a fellow in the Connecting Communities Fellowship Program sponsored by an organization called Hope in the Cities; David had been their lead consultant for several years and was a faculty member for the program. They quickly bonded around their shared interest in pushing the boundaries of dialogue and in helping groups become more efficient in addressing the issues that confront them. Around this time, David acquired his own audience polling system. After his positive exposure to the technology in the large meetings as part of AmericaSpeaks facilitation teams, he wanted to explore its use in medium-sized meetings that he facilitated on his own.

Matthew first became exposed to audience polling when he and David were together in Switzerland teaching a class on dialogue as a peace-building tool to Africans, Americans, and Europeans. When David whipped out the keypads for an evaluation session, Matthew was instantly smitten. Matthew recalls thinking that there would likely be fewer things he would enjoy more than combining group process design, public speaking, and on-the-fly data analysis. On a train ride to Zurich just after the class, the two planned their first joint audience-polling venture, which would occur at an upcoming meeting focused on promoting regional cooperation in Richmond. It was not long before Matthew acquired his own polling system, and began integrating it throughout his work.

Since we joined forces in our shared love of audience polling, we have published several articles about using instant polling to make meetings better. Whether working together or separately, we have used audience polling in a wide variety of settings. We have used polling with a handful of scientists discussing medical-testing protocols; at gatherings of conflict resolution specialists; during conferences attended by real estate agents; and at meetings with large companies that were attempting to get organizational assessments from hundreds of employees who did not have regular computer access. We have also used instantaneous polling for fun—examples include using the technology to create a judging system for a fashion show, providing group experiences at birthday parties and reunions, and delivering provocative trivia games at singles mixers.

We know that audience polling will not by itself perfect every meeting, but we continue to be amazed at its power. We remain flummoxed that more people do not realize that instant polling can turn an audience of passive observers into a room of actively engaged participants. Our hope is that this book helps spread the word about an approach to group dynamics that has changed our lives and that can change everyone's sense of what a meeting can be.

Read the Room
for Real

PART 1:
MANIFESTO

The president of the Banana Distributors Trade Association (BDTA) knew this would be a key conference. The organization, which included all the banana distributors in the country, had been reeling from recent market changes. Importation quotas had changed, allowing competition directly from Mexico. Banana prices were falling. New trucking rules were driving up shipping prices and limiting the amount of bananas that distributors could economically ship. Finally a government study was coming out claiming bananas could contribute to diabetes. The association president wanted to use the meeting to lay out her take on the problems and propose some solutions. All of these problems had developed in the last month and she had not had time to survey the membership, let alone begin to build consensus about action steps. Luckily the annual meeting was already on the docket and she could use this forum to rally the troops. If she could get enough consensus at the meeting, she could take the solutions to the Federal Trade Commission (FTC) hearing next week and begin making reforms.

As she began her speech all eyes turned to her; there was a palpable buzz in the room. As she listed the three top issues, she could feel she had the room's attention. She then made the case that the shipping problems were the top priority and immediately people turned to the person next to them. Pockets of conversation began to form and a distracting murmur started moving around the room. By the time she got to her proposed action steps half the room was no longer listening. As the session broke and people left the room the conversations grew louder and more animated. "She really nailed it," said one distributor. "Are you kidding, replied another, I'm in Texas and I'll get killed by Mexican competition." She could hear other members talking about the new study but she couldn't quite follow if they thought it was a big deal or not. As she hustled to grab a few of the larger distributors to hear their thoughts, she began to worry she had gotten it wrong. At the very least it was clear that her members weren't convinced what the biggest problem was and without unified support it was going to be hard to lobby the FTC.

An alternative to consider:

How might the president and the meeting attendees have felt leaving the meeting if the president had:

Used the meeting as an opportunity to survey the membership on their perception of top challenges to banana distributors?

and/or:

After laying out her position, asked the membership their prospective level of confidence in an association strategy emphasizing the challenges based on shipping problems?

1.
TRANSFORMING AUDIENCES INTO PARTICIPANTS

1

Transforming

Why do so many meetings have to be a waste of time? Is there anything that can be done to improve them? How can audience members feel confident that they are in the hands of a speaker who, right off the bat, has a good sense of who they are? What needs to happen so that groups leave meetings enlivened by information they could have only gotten by being present in the room? Is there something that can be done so that conference attendees do not look back on the convening as a useless endeavor that did not accomplish anything?

These are some of the questions that led us to write this book since we have a deep belief in the power and beauty of effective group meetings. Despite the frequency of meetings not living up to their potential, we are inspired by the occasions when they do allow people to fulfill their capacity for flexibility, adaptation, creativity, and innovation in addressing complex problems. Similarly, we are inspired by those occasions when meetings do in fact embody the joy of a group of people truly thinking together. Our inspiration for writing this book is the magic that happens when the group indeed becomes greater than the sum of its parts.

Chances are that most people have at least one memory of a meeting that did live up to its potential. What happened that made those meetings stand out? Was it because there was the sense that everyone had a chance for their voice to be heard? Was it because people came to the meeting with their own ideas but then left it with a greater openness to the ideas of others? Was it because people felt that everyone present was committed to building on each others' thinking and was happy to engage in the exchanges needed to create something collaboratively that they could not have created separately? Was it simply because the meeting leader conducted herself in a way that made every person feel connected to her?

Pinning down the elements of the mysterious alchemy that produces a great meeting may be difficult but most of us know what it feels like. The conclusion of all great meetings leaves participants with a sense of connectedness to each other, to those leading the meeting, and to the tasks at hand. At its best, the feeling resembles the sentiment of communion, a word that combines community and union. There is a similarity in the feeling that a great meeting produces.

The type or purpose of the meeting is less important than the outcome; the meeting could be a Midwestern region's sales team gearing up to overtake the market leader or a neighborhood meeting responding to a threatened Ku Klux Klan rally. What is significant is a similarity in the feeling that a great meeting produces: it combines a feeling of commonality among those present and a shared commitment to the collective challenge. Our intent for this book is to explain techniques we use that consistently move meetings towards that feeling of communion.

By contrast, we all are very familiar with the "draggy" feeling at the end of the meetings that do not completely collapse but never really get off the ground. This feeling seems to be highly varied in its source, and often it is hard to pin down exactly what in the meeting causes this unsatisfying feeling. Was it because of the sense that some people had something important to say that might have

> **" ...a great meeting... combines a feeling of commonality among those present and a shared commitment to the collective challenge... "**

changed the group's thinking, but did not have an opportunity to do so? Was it because many people left the room knowing that the key issues confronting the group had been avoided? Was it because it was clear that the meeting leader thought he or she was getting through but a lot of people saw the leader was overlooking clues that they were not connecting? Perhaps it was because no one had a chance to express themselves other than the people who always speak up. Or because when the meeting was over, there was a shared sense that it was unnecessary and that objectives could have been accomplished through email or other means.

WHY WE WROTE THIS BOOK

This book is focused on explaining a technology that, if used with a modicum of skill, tends to help avoid the common problems just mentioned. The technology cannot guarantee that any particular meeting will go well. However, if the technology is well-deployed, then it can increase the possibility that the meeting will provide those moments of communion when people put their hearts and minds in service towards a common way of seeing things, have a shared appreciation of each other, and unite behind a common goal.

This technology is often called instantaneous audience polling. (As we will discuss soon, we think it is time for a new and more descriptive name.) Most people have been exposed to it but have not seen it used strategically to make meetings more dynamic. Post-debate coverage of Presidential campaigns often uses this technology. Networks will commonly gather a small studio audience to watch the debate, and give each audience member a device that records their degrees of positive or negative response to each moment of the debate. The display of the group's cumulative response provides insights about the moments when the candidate was winning or losing the debate.

This technology has also been used on game shows. The once very popular quiz show "Who Wants to Be a Millionaire?" built into its structure a few "contestant lifelines" to use if a contestant was not confident of their answer. One of these lifelines was to poll the audience. The audience was presented with the question and four choices facing the contestant. After the audience weighed in, the percentages for their votes for each choice was displayed. Most estimates are that the audience chooses the correct answer over 90 percent of the time.

We believe that the core capacity of this technology—to ask each person in a group a question and display an instant summary of the collective response—adds a dynamic flow that can turn average meetings into good ones and good meetings into great ones. If used even minimally, the technology can add a bit of entertaining and unpredictable pizzazz to what would otherwise be a conventional meeting experience. If used at its utmost, the technology causes a significant shift in what the meeting is. The collective response to questions becomes a core element in the meeting—one that can influence what presenters say, what the meeting attendees talk about, the flow of the meeting through the agenda, and what are considered the key takeaways from the convening. In this way, polling technology can potentially transform a meeting from an experience of pre-scripted theater where the presenter is an actor on a stage and the crowd is an audience to one that is a facilitated and organic encounter, where both the presenter and the audience are each co-participants in creating a group experience whose outcome builds group momentum in a way that is not completely understood in advance.

We want to foster a change so that fewer meetings are presenter-centric and more of them are participant-centered. This can never happen completely, because the need for a coherent plan and flow means that someone will always be making the decision about

> **"...if used at its utmost, the technology causes a significant shift in what the meeting is. The collective response to questions becomes a core element in the meeting..."**

the pace of events and attention during the meeting. Even if the continuity of the meeting is dependent on participant answers to polling queries, someone will be designing the questions. So there are limits to how participant-centered a meeting can be, especially if it involves more than a handful of people. But currently, the activities of most meetings of any size are far too centered on the perspective of meeting presenters and sponsors. People who plan meetings may (or may not) put a lot of effort into anticipating the perspective of the participants and then constructing a meeting that fulfills these objectives in a way that accommodates this guess about what participants will be thinking. Hence, there is a significant amount of work that goes into planning a meeting in addition to an equal amount of guesswork that results.

If the meeting planner's assessment of what the participants think is off the mark, the signals about this fact may be hard to read, so they do not know whether any adjustments are needed. Many people who care about meetings are not aware that there is a technology that allows meeting presenters and sponsors to know with good precision what meeting attendees are thinking, and to do so at any point in a meeting. This new capability, if fully utilized, makes it possible to lessen disconnects between those who arranged the meeting and those who attended it. The people organizing the meeting can know with much greater clarity how close they are coming to fulfilling their meeting objectives. In addition, this capacity also allows meeting attendees to more clearly see how their perspective on relevant issues fits within the entire group, and thus helps people feel more connected to each other and to opportunities and challenges facing the group.

For the first time in the long history of people gathering, everyone in a meeting can know with clarity what meeting attendees have been through, what they think right now, and what they want to do. In our opinion, this is a potential paradigm shift in what a meeting can be, and builds upon previous shifts that we have come to think of as natural. Namely, sound amplification allows everyone in a meeting to clearly hear the thoughts of a speaker; the projector allowed all those who attend a meeting to see a visual depiction the speaker thinks is helpful. Audience polling builds upon these previous developments in that now everyone can get a visual depiction of the summary of everyone's thoughts.

From a technological standpoint, this technology is old; from the standpoint of the hundreds of thousands of years that people have struggled to make collective decisions, this capability is very new.

We think this shift in what meetings can be will turn out to be very significant, and we write this book to persuade readers that this shift is something to be heartily embraced, and aggressively disseminated. We also write this book to offer our practical, perhaps even picky, advice about the key steps, some of them very small, that are useful in creating the meeting magic that the technology makes possible.

The purpose of this book is to persuade readers that this technology can give meetings a level of dynamism and electricity for those who attend them, run them, and pay for them. In order to help you create great meetings using this technology, we will pass along some of the lessons we have learned about getting the most out of this tool so that meeting objectives are fulfilled, but are done so in a way that is better for everyone.

The book combines a call to action, some detailed instructions, and some contemplation of the long-term implications. In Part 1: Manifesto, we discuss the technology in a way that explains why it can function as a transformative force in meetings; our intention is to invite the reader to join us as early adopters of the new paradigm. In Part 2, we provide a Users Manual about the technology. We explore with some specificity how one uses polling in different types of meetings. We also provide guidance about how the technology can be used to add a special type of magic to social events. In Part 3: Reflections, we offer our thinking about the influences affecting the dissemination of the technology, the people we think should most immediately start using it, and the underlying values it embodies. Depending on your role in your organization or in meetings, you may want to focus on one part or another in this book.

Our appreciation of the technology comes in some measure because we have gone to a lot of meetings in our lifetimes. Before becoming meeting strategists, we spent a lot of time in academic environments, which are replete with meetings, both great and wearisome. We went to relatively prestigious undergraduate colleges (Princeton and William and Mary) and between us have two Masters degrees and a doctorate. As facilitators, we have organized meetings for a wide range of clients, including top elected officials such as the President, Members of Congress, and big city mayors. Our corporate clients have included Fortune 500 firms, such as Wells Fargo, MadeWaco, Genworth, Silicon Graphics, and Capital One. Our philanthropic clients have included foundations such as the Kellogg Foundation, the Annie E. Casey Foundation, and the Sherwood Foundation. Some of our non-profit clients have included international peace organizations, museums, and national associations. Between the meetings we have created and those we have observed, we have attended hundreds of events of all types. Our cumulative experience has led us both to believe that audience polling is severely underused, considering its potential value.

This book explains how this technology can improve meetings by helping participants engage more directly, by ensuring that presenters know more about their audience, and by providing meeting sponsors with more usable data from the gatherings they pay for. This book will also demonstrate the way that this technology can have the unexpected effect of pushing participants, presenters, and sponsors to ask useful, reflective questions about their own goals for any meeting.

"...our cumulative experience has led us both to believe that audience polling is severely underused, considering its potential value..."

SOME BACKGROUND

The capacity to conduct an audience poll that queries and hears from every person directly and relatively quickly has been around since at least the early 1970s. However, advances in computer and communications technology, software interfaces, and mass production over the last decade have made the latest generation of devices simpler to use, easier to store and transport, and much cheaper. In fact, in the past seven or so years, a number of companies have begun offering services that are based not on separate hand-held devices that have to be distributed and collected, but rather driven by responses from telephones, tablets, or laptops that participants have brought to the meeting. With many people carrying around such devices, it is getting significantly easier to conduct instantaneous polling of an audience in a way that makes meetings better for everyone.

In response to these rapid advances in the accessibility of audience polling, the education sector—from kindergarten through graduate school—is beginning to leverage the many benefits of audience polling. There is good evidence that polling fosters greater attention by students as well as greater retention of concepts and facts. Driven primarily by teacher use, audience polling has grown dramatically over the past several years. Futuresource, a leading research firm on the audience polling market, estimates that 2.3 million handheld devices were sold in the United States in 2013, with another 600,000 being sold beyond its borders. One executive at a large company publicly stated that total sales of audience polling devices stands at roughly 15 million worldwide. Our hope is that over time the benefits of audience polling will spread to non-classroom meetings.

There are a number of forces or drivers that are also pushing in the direction of increased use of the technology to improve meetings. Although these forces have been in place for many years, the penetration of audience polling within the adult-meeting market—for trainings, speeches, facilitated workshops, and conferences—is still relatively small. The two main reasons for this are that many people have not seen the devices or software, or have not seen them used strategically for the purpose of making meetings better. Our aim is to change that.

YOUTH > Polling is being introduced at younger ages which makes the classroom experience interactive and potentially benefits the student in the long run as skills become transferable once they are of working age.

FREQUENCY > Surveys and polling frequency are becoming increasingly more common whether they occur on television shows, websites, personal devices, or from businesses wanting feedback.

CULTURE CHANGE > The use of handheld devices and technology during face-to-face encounters with other people is becoming more acceptable.

ECONOMICS > Managers are asking harder questions about whether the costs of in-person meetings are worth the expense, which creates more pressure for meetings to produce tangible results.

"...the penetration of audience polling within the adult-meeting market...is still relatively small...our aim is to change that."

WHOM THIS BOOK IS FOR

This book is written for people who create meetings on an ad hoc basis, including:
- Managers who are interested in improving the quality of the meetings they attend or convene,
- Urban planners,
- Community organizers,
- Civic or community engagement specialists,
- Public officials (elected or appointed) and their staffs,
- Conflict resolution professionals, and
- Party and reunion planners.

It is also written for people who make meetings happen all the time, including:
- Trainers whose aim is to deliver specific technical content,
- Speakers whose intention is to inspire, motivate, and/or entertain,
- Facilitators whose focus is getting audience members to engage with one another, and perhaps to elicit information from audience members,
- Conference and meeting planners whose aim is to make provisions for a gathering that includes two or more connected meetings, and
- Information technology managers and audio/visual specialists particularly those who enjoy thinking about the content of meetings.

While we are passionate advocates of audience polling as a way of improving a wide variety of gatherings, we are not zealots. We will discuss the fact that more participant engagement also raises questions about the level of unpredictability in a meeting, as well as the issue of who gets to control what happens during a meeting. The capacity for giving participants greater voice in meetings can be a catalyst for more participation. We will discuss the fact that this capability only heightens questions about power and control over what happens during a gathering.

WHAT THIS BOOK IS AND IS NOT

We wrote this book to accomplish two primary purposes. First, we wanted to expose people outside the education/academic sector to the often overlooked but nevertheless tremendous value that audience polling can provide. (In the bibliography, you will find references to several books that highlight the use of polling devices in the classroom; this has not been our specialty). Second, we wanted to give some guidance so that people who plan meetings can take maximum advantage of the available technology.

To our way of thinking, the penetration of audience polling into the adult meeting market should be more extensive than it currently is. As meeting strategists we do not care whether the market for audience polling technology grows into one with a wide range of companies each with small market share (such as is the case with the laptop industry) or into a very small number of companies that dominate the field (as in the case with the market for air travel). As long as people are having better meetings, we do not care how the market sorts itself out.

That said, it is important to know that both of us are long-term customers of a company called Turning Technologies, which makes audience polling systems. We are both considered "distinguished users" of their products. For a number of years running, this company has been talked about as the dominant player in the audience polling market. The fact that we are long-term users of this company's polling systems also means that we may talk about capabilities of polling systems that products of other companies do not have; it also may be that there are useful capabilities of those polling systems that we will fail to mention because we do not know about them.

As much as we want to promote the use of polling, our intention here is not to give you guidance about how to evaluate products. At some point, we may examine a number of products and produce a buyer's guide. This book does not attempt to serve that purpose.

This book is also not intended to be a thorough compendium of research about audience polling devices, although we do include several references in a few key places.

The aim of this book is to enable the reader to make choices about how they engage a myriad of participants, be they consumers of a meeting, customers with whom the meeting convener has a long-going relationship, counselors who offer valued advice, or collaborators who are thought of as partners. Certainly, our intention is to discuss the ways that this technology allows a meeting convener to better engage each of these types of stakeholders. Even more than that, we think that this technology raises profound questions about how these group relationships are regarded. In this age of technological overload and saturation, any stakeholder meeting should not waste people's time. Our hope is to make it likely that any gathering has resonance of the magical feeling that can happen when people are fully exploring their collective wisdom and will.

> **"...this technology raises profound questions about how these group relationships are regarded."**

> **NOTE:** For those wanting an excellent bibliography on the use of audience response devices, Derek Bruff has provided one which can be found at: http://cft.vanderbilt.edu/docs/classroom-response-system-clickers-bibliography/#psych

To thoroughly discuss the ways that audience polling makes meetings better, here are some terms we will use:

MEETING PROFESSIONAL: any person who has the regular responsibility of thinking about the logistics of meetings. This term is intended to include speakers, meeting or conference planners who work independently, people who rent out meeting space, professional facilitators, event planners and anyone else who regularly organizes gatherings.

MEETING ORGANIZER: the person who has primary responsibility for making a particular meeting happen.

MEETING STRATEGIST: the person who is focused primarily on the process and the content of the meeting, and is thinking about how the content relates to the desired meeting outcomes.

PRESENTER: a person who, for all or a portion of a meeting, is the primary person in front of a group managing the session. This person could be a speaker, panel moderator, trainer, or workshop facilitator.

POLLING FACILITATOR: the person who is leading a group through polling questions. Usually, this person is also the presenter, but sometimes a polling facilitator simply manages the polling process before returning control to a presenter who is not doing polling.

MEETING SPONSOR/CLIENT: the person or group who hires a meeting organizer or sits on a committee that authorizes the payment of a meeting organizer.

AUDIENCE POLLING SYSTEM: the term that signifies the input devices, the receiver, the computer, the projector, and even the sound system that creates the interactive experience. Audience polling systems are often referred to as audience response systems (ARS), personal response devices, or other terms. We suggest a new name below.

KEYPADS/CLICKERS: the handheld devices that people use to register their vote on an audience polling system.

KEYPAD SYSTEM/CLICKER SYSTEM: same as audience polling systems.

NOTE: In some cases, the organizer, strategist, presenter, facilitator, and sponsor are all the same people; in others, each of these roles is comprised of separate teams of folks.

WHO WE ARE

Like many consultants, we are willing to claim a number of areas of expertise: facilitation, dialogue, conflict resolution, civic engagement, diversity, racial inclusion, organizational development, strategic planning, and so on. One skill that we are known somewhat widely for is using the audience polling systems to enhance meetings, conferences, panel discussions, and other types of gatherings. We have demonstrated the benefits of polling in a variety of settings that have ranged from several people gathered around a table to several thousand people at multiple meetings linked by satellite. As we have done this, we usually try to serve as meeting strategists, which enables us to consciously implement the meeting in light of our client's objectives and perhaps beyond those. But sometimes, we just run the polling equipment, and because it always makes meetings better, that limited role is fine too.

While we often work together in our mission of changing the world one polling question at a time, we also operate separately with our own individual consulting practices. For the sake of this book, we will adopt the conceit that all of our projects were joint efforts; this will make language simpler as we refer to our past endeavors.

In the literature about meetings, audience polling systems are most commonly referred to as audience response systems, or ARS for short. We do not like this name. First, it sounds too much like British slang for a body part. Second, when referring to the entire system, the name "ARS system" pushes toward redundancy, like "ATM machine." This technology needs an acronym that makes sense both when it is spoken and when it is spelled out.

For those reasons, we suggest that a renaming of this technology is needed. We want to suggest that people talking about the technology and the systems that implement audience polling refer to it as providing SPEIK (Speed Polling to Enhance Input and Knowledge). While we sometimes still use terms like "keypads" or "clickers" for the hand-held devices, SPEIK as a term is closer, we think, to conveying what the technology does by giving everyone a voice in the meeting. And it makes sense to talk about "SPEIK devices", "SPEIK systems", "SPEIK technology" and "SPEIK capability."

S P E I K
Speed Polling to Enhance Input and Knowledge

Leona Hart was excited to present at the Banana Distributors Trade Association (BDTA) national meeting. For the last six months she had been developing a new member opinion tracking system for the association. As a growing organization, the BDTA needed to stay on top of its membership's concerns and the new system would allow each distributor to respond to survey questions on a weekly basis. Hart believed the lukewarm reception of the BDTA President's speech proved the need for the tracking system.

Her presentation focused on the technical alternatives she had evaluated and how to address the issue of system compatibility. In all she had 16 major technical points to cover. She also needed to describe how the program was being funded and the implementation efforts that the distributors would need to make. The BDTA President had specifically asked for these last two points but Hart was less familiar with these issues and she had put them at the end of the talk in the hope that she would not get too many questions.

Hart began her talk by mentioning how increased data was changing the world before jumping into the difficulties of developing a coordinated and linked computer system to aggregate data. By the time she got to the choice of software packages there seemed to be a fair amount of side conversations. Realizing she may need to slow down, she asked if there were any questions. One of the distributors who she was working with on system testing asked a "softball" question about the user interface model and Hart brought up a screen shot of the interface to help the audience see how user friendly the system was.

With her time running out she realized she had not gotten into the funding mechanism or the distributor responsibilities for uploading their survey responses. As people began to get up to leave she flipped to the slides on these points and read the bullet points. "If you have any questions, please find me," she said, as the session ended.

An alternative to consider:

How might the analyst and the meeting attendees have felt if the analyst had incorporated SPEIK and:

Asked the attendees to express if they understood the intention of the new system?

and/or:

Asked attendees to assess their interest and willingness in participating in the system?

2.
THE IMPACT OF SPEIK ON PEOPLE WHO PLAN, PAY FOR, PRESENT AT, AND ATTEND MEETINGS

2

Impact

Americans go to a lot of meetings. According to an often cited 1989 study by Hofstra University, wasted time in meetings costs the economy more than $37 billion a year. While much of this is for small meetings that only include a handful of people, our own experience in talking to groups about meetings is that the phenomenon of wasting time in poorly run meetings is a perception shared by people in the corporate, government, and military sectors, and by people of all age groups and types. This happens for many reasons: poor facilitation, people showing up late, lack of needed data or people being in the room, and so on.

Our sense is that a primary reason for the perception and reality of wasted time in meetings is that meeting strategists—the people whose charge is to ensure that the meeting content and process support the sponsors' and organizers' objectives—do not think hard enough or clearly enough about the purposes of this very expensive thing called a meeting. While SPEIK cannot solve this problem by itself, we have found that the capacity to ask everyone a question and very quickly know the collective range of participant answers tends to push meeting strategists to think more clearly about the fundamental question that people who plan meetings should continually revisit: What should be the primary activity of this moment in the meeting so that it best advances the meeting's objectives?

> **NOTE:** The following schema of three modes of communication in meetings is a variant of the seven-mode workshop model used by Sam Kaner in *A Facilitator's Guide to Participatory Decision Making (2007)*, a widely cited handbook about workshop facilitation.[1]

We wrestle with this issue constantly, and it seems that a useful way of addressing the answers to this question is to think of meeting moments as embodying some combination (usually one at any specific moment) of three different modes of interaction: Download, Feedback, and Crosstalk.

DOWNLOAD MODE
ONE PERSON COMMUNICATES TO MANY PEOPLE
"I want them to understand me."

In this mode, the primary objective of the meeting leader is to get the central points across to the audience. Examples of meetings dominated by this mode are trainings, classes, TED Talks, panel discussions, and banquet speeches, as well as an organizational leader making a speech at the annual company gathering, and so on. The content might be facts, concepts, stories, emotions, or other issues, but the core purpose of that moment in the meeting is to

MODE CHARACTERISTICS:

SUCCESS FACTORS:

High level of participant absorption of specific facts, concepts, techniques, or feelings.

FAILURE SOURCES:

- The presenter(s) deliver their information based on a significant misunderstanding of the perspective of the audience, so the presenter does not connect with them.
- The session ends without the presenter getting information that confirms that people have absorbed the intended message.

SPEIK OUTCOMES:

- Presenters can know what the audience thinks and adjust the presentation accordingly
- Presenters can measure the degree to which they have achieved their goals in participant understanding

get some type of information from the presenter into the minds of the audience. Typically, the reason the group is going through the expense and hassles of convening is because someone has decided that it is vital that the entire group hear the same message and have a common experience.

If used well, SPEIK is able to address these sources of failure by allowing the presenter to read the room accurately either on the front end or back end of the presentation. SPEIK can assess with precision the level of participant comprehension of the content, which gives presenters the capacity to make adjustments if needed and if possible, do so on the fly. As we will discuss in chapter 4, SPEIK questions tend to increase the learning of facts by meeting attendees. (In chapter 5 we will provide some detailed practical advice about how to get the most out of the technology for speeches, panel discussions, training, and other common download focused meetings.)

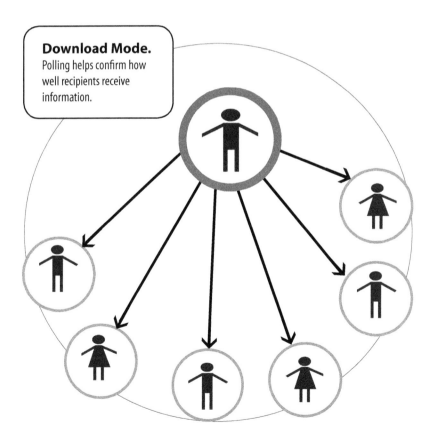

Download Mode.
Polling helps confirm how well recipients receive information.

2.1

Every year, an annual conference brings meteorologists to Lake Tahoe to discuss the latest developments in weather forecasting, findings in climate science, and the future of the region. In 2013, we served as an interactive warm-up act just before an address by one of the world's top climate scientists, Dr. William Collins. Our design strategy in creating a 12-minute polling experience was to ask questions that would let both the scientist and the audience get a good sense of who was in the room. Questions concerned issues such as: how many of the audience were residents versus tourists, participants' favorite local recreational activities, and their beliefs about the issue of human-caused climate change. Twice during his speech, Dr. Collins mentioned his gratitude in knowing that more than 85 percent of the crowd believed in man-made climate change; he said that he was happy to know the group's views were aligned with his own, and that he need not spend time persuading the group about this point. He said that he appreciated knowing that he could instead focus on conveying strategies that people could use to build the local and national movement to change public policy.

" SPEIK gives presenters the capacity to make adjustments...and do so on the fly. "

A second focus of communication—which, like the other modes discussed, can sometimes comprise the purpose of the entire meeting—is to solicit the perspectives of the audience about some concept, situation, fact, or possibility, in order to augment the thinking or decision-making of a decision-maker. It only makes sense to engage in this exchange if some decision-makers have decided that their thinking is improved by engaging what might be called the "group mind", with the hopefully diverse perspectives contained in it. This is what happens when the President of the United States gathers the cabinet to get each of their perspectives

MODE CHARACTERISTICS:

SUCCESS FACTORS:

After the meeting, the presenter has an accurate and true assessment of the range of candid perspectives of the participants on the topics of relevance.

FAILURE SOURCES:

- Some participants are reluctant to provide their candid perspective.
- Sometimes aggressive participants can dominate the process, leaving a distorted impression of the range or mix of viewpoints present.

SPEIK OUTCOMES:

- Increases the number of people whose views have been captured.
- Increase in honest responses because of anonymity.
- Heightened awareness that differences in perception and opinions are healthy.
- Greater ability to tally responses creates more accurate understanding of the diversity of participant viewpoints.

before making a decision on a controversial issue, or when people convene focus groups so they can better calibrate a strategy. Other examples of feedback sessions are listening sessions by politicians, meetings where a company's personnel help management think about a new initiative from different points of view, or when a planner or governmental agency official convenes a meeting to hear from a neighborhood. In these situations, a decision-maker wants input from top advisers or even a larger set of relevant stakeholders, but reserves the options for decision to him or herself. The purpose of the gathering is to arrange a meeting in largely feedback mode to get a variety of perspectives.

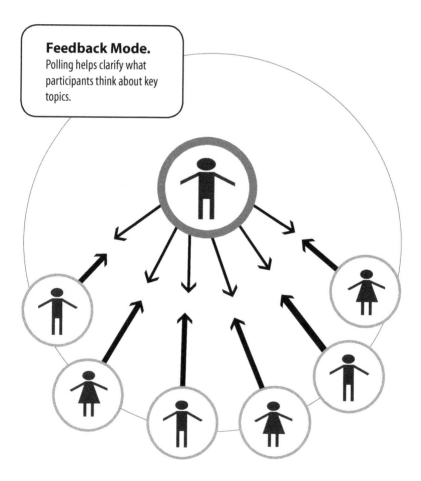

Feedback Mode.
Polling helps clarify what participants think about key topics.

Every summer, the SKILLZ Summer School program in Pasadena California runs an 8-week summer school to help young people, mostly from poor neighborhoods, make up for academic deficiencies that will prevent them from advancing in school. We were asked to create an interactive experience that would be energizing but would also help the staff and the students to understand the challenges they would be facing during the summer. In addition to fun questions such as "Which place has the best burgers?", the polling queries included questions such as: "How often do your parents help you with your homework?" and "Which of these recreational drugs have you taken in the last 30 days?". Some of the information gleaned from the anonymous polling results—such as the portion of the youth who had purposely tried to hurt themselves—was not only eye opening to the program staff, but also affected the grant strategy of SKILLZ Summer School for the next year.

CROSSTALK MODE
MANY COMMUNICATE TO MANY
"I want them to understand each other."

The third crosstalk mode is one in which the group interacts with each other and, hopefully, comes to a higher understanding of something important because of the collaborative communication process. Of the three modes it is the most complex. Examples of this are retreats, workshops that are not trainings, meetings where a group

MODE CHARACTERISTICS:

SUCCESS FACTORS:

The extent to which the group's communication is honest, fully considers all of the relevant factors, is collaborative and actually advances the groups collective understanding of its situation.

FAILURE SOURCES:

- People do not say what they really think.
- People become very attached to their own perspective, and do not see other perspectives as valuable.
- Past issues of distrust or other negative feelings affect people's willingness to engage authentically.
- The meeting spends too much time on issues that are not central to its current predicament.

SPEIK OUTCOMES:

- Fosters greater connectedness between people before they start to wrangle with issues that divide them.
- Provides a safe outlet for people to raise difficult issues without initially identifying themselves as doing so.
- Helps people see their perspective as one of many possible viewpoints, which often makes them less attached to their position.
- Helps a group make good decisions about which issues to spend time on.
- Helps a group identify the "low-hanging fruit" of agreement that might merit immediate focus.

makes a decision, board meetings, and so on. This is the realm of the discussion, dialogue, and sometimes decision-making where the "presenter" serves as a catalyst to help the group share information, find their common motivation, progress through existing conflicts, define key problems, identify preferred solutions, and the like.

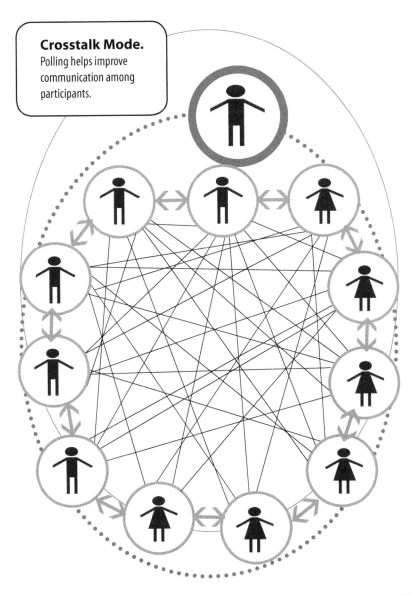

Crosstalk Mode.
Polling helps improve communication among participants.

Environmental activists in the historically African-American Bayview-Hunter's Point section of San Francisco have a history of tense relationships with institutional authorities, since they believe that many decisions have been made that have harmed the area and the health of its residents. A few years ago, a local quasi-government authority with responsibility for air quality was planning on dispensing up to $500,000 to address health problems related to air quality. In an attempt to shift to a more cooperative dynamic with local community activists, the agency engaged us to design some participatory meetings with neighborhood residents. These meetings would potentially allow residents to weigh in on dilemmas related to spending the funds, such as whether the money should go to increased regulation of dry cleaners versus increased screenings for asthma. Although there were initial plans to picket the meeting, local activists eventually decided to participate after they were convinced that there would be no attempts to stifle community perspectives. At various points in the small group discussions, SPEIK technology was used to help the group see its collective view of the key health problems, to sort out its sense of underlying air quality problems, and to discern which approaches to using the expected funds garnered the most support.

A few closing points about this framework for thinking about meetings.

One point about this framework that some people have found useful is that there are often disconnects between what meeting strategists want and what participants expect. The classic version of this is a setting where the meeting has been planned to be a download session and attendees arrive with the expectation of providing feedback. Frustration usually ensues. A similar frustration happens when meeting attendees expect that a meeting will involve communication and collective decision making, and it turns out that the decision-maker primarily wants feedback and is reserving the decision-making authority for him- or herself. It is important not only to be clear about what mode a session comprises, but valuable to be transparent as well.

A different problem besides clarity and transparency but one that can nevertheless undermine meetings is a gap between what a meeting organizer wants and the processes they use to achieve those outcomes. For example, many meetings are intended to allow the decision-maker to get feedback from a gathering of people, but the structure of the meeting (for example, an open mic that allows a sequence of short statements by some attendees) is not well-suited to create a clear picture of the true perspective of the group. In such a setting, it is easy for a few voices to dominate, and the decision-makers to not get a clear picture of the group's opinion.

A related problem occurs when a decision-maker wants to engage in some collaborative examination with a board or cabinet of less powerful advisors. Unless close attention is paid to the process used for engaging the group, people may be reluctant to express themselves before they know they have support; thus, the decision-maker may not achieve the intended goals of getting honest input. Another common mistake that meeting organizers make is to have the intention of holding a session of crosstalk, but give precious little thought to creating a process by which people can really engage each other and potentially influence each other's thinking and come to collective conclusions.

In making the distinctions between the meeting modes above, we are not suggesting that meetings or moments in meetings always fall neatly into one of these three modes. Often meetings merge and meld these different types of objectives; sometimes they do this well, and many times poorly. Most of the large meetings we have facilitated have used the three modes at different stages. The participants were told some relevant information, were encouraged to give feedback on some other issues that the decision-makers retained control over, and on a third set of items, participants were empowered to arrive at conclusions that would be directly followed-up with actions.

Though actual meetings often blend these modes, some patterns exist worth highlighting, and the rest of the text will often reflect this. As our discussion of polling continues, we will usually talk about deploying SPEIK in three meeting types: 1) speeches and panels that are largely download mode, 2) conferences that are largely feedback mode, and 3) workshops that are largely crosstalk mode. The critical point to remember about the modes is that regardless of the type of meeting, it is important for meeting strategists and the presenter to be clear about the intention of the communication they are trying to support at any moment.

If you integrate these modes well, people often come away from a meeting very invigorated, largely because they have an intuitive sense that at many moments, the tremendous cost of meetings was being matched by a sense that something important was happening that could not have happened if folks were not in the same room. They will feel that at almost every moment, the meeting had a purpose, and that their presence mattered.

A very important impact of SPEIK is that it tends to nudge meeting strategists toward a greater degree of discipline in their thinking about the meeting. The strategist tends to ask him- or herself: how would seeing the thoughts of the group help the meeting objectives? This question raises the associated question: what are the key objectives of this moment?

Given how many meetings wander from lack of a clear agenda and do not have processes appropriate to their objectives, this tendency to foster greater clarity on the part of meeting strategists is very valuable in itself. In addition, there are effects of SPEIK on other key stakeholders in the meeting that are worth exploring in a full inventory of what SPEIK does to/for the process of planning, delivering, and learning from meetings.

THE IMPACT OF POLLING ON MEETING SPONSORS

There are times when SPEIK is deployed because the sponsor has a vital need for information that can only be attained by surveying the group. Depending on the purpose of the meeting, the sponsor may need this information for tactical choices such as future meeting locations or key strategic decisions about a group or institution's behavior. We have been involved in many meetings where polling data was used to help guide policy decisions of large public agencies.

*SPEIK technology can sometimes
generate information that is
not just helpful, but is vital for
decision-making.*

2.4

In 2002, AmericaSpeaks brought together 4,500 people to review draft plans to rebuild the World Trade Center site. Six different conceptual plans developed by the planning team hired by the Lower Manhattan Development Corporation (LMDC) were presented to the public. After several hours of discussion followed by polling, participants in "Listening to the City" overwhelmingly rejected all of the originally proposed plans. Some common complaints were that the plans were too dense, too dull, and too commercial. As a result of the clarity generated by the meeting, LMDC threw out the original plans and sponsored a worldwide design competition whose framework was in part based on the vision and principles the public developed and embraced during the meeting.

In this example (2.4), the sponsor engaged a meeting organizer in part because of the organization's ability to use audience polling (and other group processes) to generate information for decision-making. However, this is not the only circumstance when data produced from audience polling affects management decisions.

*SPEIK sometimes inadvertently
creates information that can
benefit meeting sponsors.*

2.5

At an annual women-in-business conference in Richmond, Virginia, we deployed SPEIK as a way of helping the conference attendees learn who else was attending. The conference organizer, a minority business association, also wanted to collect demographic information, such as organizational position held, size and type of organization represented, and annual salary of participants. After the conference, the organizers created a marketing packet with the profile of their conference participants. They later told us that having this information helped them successfully increase their sponsors for the next year.

In the World Trade Center example (2.4), the sponsor was committed to acquiring polling data on group preferences as soon as the planning began; in the business association case (2.5), audience polling inadvertently elicited information that group decision-makers chose to consider as part of its on-going management.

*SPEIK can cause sponsors to
revisit opportunities to leverage
the meeting that had not been
initially considered.*

There is a third way in which SPEIK can affect a sponsor's strategic thinking: when a meeting sponsor wants polling and is not considering the potential value of the data for decisions, but the discipline of planning for clearly defined polling questions (in either download, feedback, or crosstalk mode) pushes the sponsor to think more strategically about additional possibilities for what can happen at the meeting.

If you are a meeting professional who is assessing the pros and cons of becoming familiar with the technology, this third scenario is important to consider.

2.6

A university had engaged us to do some meeting design and facilitation of a community engagement process to help influence a nascent community health campaign. They had heard of our previous work in using SPEIK to make meetings more engaging, and were excited about implementing it. During the first meeting with a small committee of university staff, we began to ask basic questions that had to do with the purpose of the first community meeting: What are the best-case outcomes from the meeting? Is the purpose of the meeting to try to start a dialogue with community members in order to generate ideas, or is the goal to get feedback on ideas the university already has about the campaign? Who will make decisions about this campaign, or even about the meeting to define it?

After we asked these questions, it became clear to us and to the client that the university was unsure about its strategy for engaging the community. As a result, the client decided that in order for the community meeting to effectively shape the upcoming engagement campaign, it was important to have community voices involved in the committee to plan the initial meeting. The university moved to significantly increase the size of the committee, and to populate it with equal numbers of university staff and community members. The committee redefined our contract from simply doing one meeting to helping them think through and execute the planning phase of a broader community engagement campaign that would involve many more opportunities for community input.

" SPEIK pushes the sponsor to think more strategically about what can happen at the meeting. "

Why does SPEIK force more discipline in meeting planning?

There is no guarantee that a meeting sponsor who thinks only about making a meeting more dynamic will subsequently move to contemplating the role of participant input in management decisions. But such a transition is not uncommon. Here's why:

Audience polling forces a level of discipline on the meeting strategist who is crafting the polling questions and positioning them on the meeting agenda. No matter which type of communication is being augmented by polling, on the day of the meeting, the strategist must have fully developed a set of specific polling questions with specific optional responses; he or she will have used his or her best judgment to determine when is the best time in the agenda for each question.

In order to prepare polling questions that have a good chance of achieving the best impacts on the participants and on the presenter described above, the meeting strategist will have to contemplate two questions:

REQUIRED QUESTIONS FOR STRATEGISTS:

What are engaging polling questions that might be perceived by participants as enjoyable, interesting, or positive?

What are polling questions that might help the presenter/facilitator more effectively read the group in a way that pursues meeting goals at that moment?

Most experienced meeting strategists can create a decent draft of polling questions that address these issues by knowing the background of the group, the purpose of the meeting, and the meeting content. Of course, it will be important to have the strategist's judgment validated by the client; before the polling session begins, he or she will in all likelihood have orchestrated some communication with the sponsor to approve the questions and their timing.

However, unless the strategist knows the sponsoring group and its management very well, he or she will be much less likely to develop questions that the sponsor will consider useful in management decisions that are outside the original scope of the meeting. Such useful information could come from interpretations of recent group events, internal trends, external dynamics, and prospects for the future—the list of possibilities is endless. If the organizer wants to create polling questions that have practical value to the sponsor, the meeting strategist will have to engage the sponsor (or designee) in a version of a third question:

OPTIONAL QUESTION A STRATEGIST CAN ASK:

What polling questions might generate information that will help the group advance its objectives, either for this meeting or in a broader context?

A meeting strategist who is hired to make a gathering more dynamic through using SPEIK is not required to present the sponsor with the opportunity to make the meeting more productive in other ways. And even if the organizer raises this possibility, the sponsor may not want to have this conversation, for any number of reasons (for example, management confusion, internal organizational tensions, historical dynamics in the organization, and so on).

In many instances, the sponsor will be at least somewhat open to the idea of exploring questions that might add additional value to the meeting. Sometimes, new questions that will be potentially useful to the sponsor will be readily apparent. There are many times, however, when the sponsor needs to be guided through the process of thinking through the potential value of polling the meeting participants on other topics. It may be a shift for them to think of the gathering as an opportunity to leverage the brainpower of the group by getting additional feedback from it; in this circumstance, the meeting strategist is essentially coaching the sponsor to see that the meeting is a resource that can be used to help with decision-making.

If the strategist opens up the optional question, above, and the sponsor does not have ready answers but is intrigued about the possibilities, the strategist organizer will probably need to ask some additional clarifying questions, such as:

ADDITIONAL QUESTIONS A STRATEGIST CAN ASK:

What are the purposes of this meeting?

How do the purposes of this particular meeting relate to the sponsors' broader objectives for the group?

What data is needed that will help improve decision-making that advances the goals of the meeting?

Are there polling questions that might generate data useful for some group objectives that are not related to the original purpose of the meeting?

To some meeting professionals, opening up an exploratory discussion with the client along these lines may be undesirable because the conversation seems like too much work, or because it takes the meeting professional away from their core passions or skill set. To others, going the extra mile in this manner is an easy way for a meeting professional to add perceived value to the interaction with the sponsor. By expanding the vetting of engagement-oriented polling questions to an exploration of what polling questions might be more generally effective, the meeting professional is evolving into a more broadly thinking meeting strategist, and perhaps even into a strategic advisor to the sponsor beyond the meeting.

THE IMPACT OF POLLING ON MEETING PRESENTERS

One reason that SPEIK is commonly rated as a highlight of meetings is that it boosts the energy of the event by strengthening the connection between participants and presenters. By allowing the presenter to read the room very precisely, SPEIK data puts the presenter in a position to manipulate the meeting management with minor and sometimes major changes. If the presenter does a good job of making these subtle or substantial modifications, participants will often feel that the presenter is more responsive to them, further boosting the connection between the two.

> SPEIK creates an inherently spontaneous moment of connection between presenter and participants.

2.7   **Only a few weeks before a long-planned conference of 800 real estate professionals and scholars, we were engaged to conduct keypad polling at various points.** To prepare the polling sessions for each panel discussion, we had to have a conversation with each moderator to gain a basic understanding of each speaker's content; we then designed questions that would be relevant to the panelists' contributions. On the day of the conference, the experts often altered their prepared assessment and projections about relevant markets and trends in a way that framed their observations in light of the SPEIK results. The polling information helped the panels become a setting where each speaker engaged in conversation with the participants in the room, instead of a setting where panelists merely delivered their planned presentation and answered questions from a few members of the audience.

Debra Jarvis
Retired Fire Chief
Public Safety Consultant and Conference Presenter

Ms. Jarvis participated in a SPEIK demonstration at a conference focused on diversity and inclusion.

I go to a lot of conferences and make presentations at a lot of conferences. I am rarely wowed. When I saw the demonstration, I was wowed! These devices are amazing. As instructor, you can think you have a pulse on what is happening, but you might not actually know. This is a great way of knowing what people are thinking about that they might not be willing to say.

2.8

    Before a meeting we facilitated with 120 people who had been concerned about a large municipal library, there had been a fair amount of community disagreement about how well the library was serving the needs of different sub-populations. We conducted audience polling at the start of the meeting that helped clarify that there was broad agreement in the room: the library was doing a good job of serving college-educated adults and children who were at less than appropriate reading levels. There was also broad agreement among attendees that the library's service to teenagers was poor. However, the polling showed that there was significant disagreement about whether the library was providing good service to adults with significant literacy deficits. Knowing this information allowed us to take the discussion of the groups being served well off the agenda. We then quickly advanced to brainstorming strategies about the teenage population and on to constructing a dialogue to probe different views on how well the library was serving adults with literacy deficiencies.

Later in the book we will review some ideas about the keys to constructing good questions. For now, suffice it to say that SPEIK questions have impact as long as questions are designed so that they are relevant to the meeting purpose and help create some unexpected learning about the diverse ways that the participants relate to each other and their common objectives. When this happens reasonably well, the meeting presenter's attention is shifted to the findings in the room, which gives the meeting a sense of increased vibrancy.

THE IMPACT OF POLLING ON MEETING PARTICIPANTS

A polling question can be thought of as three actions in rapid sequence: the group's attention is directed to a question, people register their response, and the group's attention is directed to a graphic summarizing the group's response. This is how this sequence effects participants:

The polling process increases the amount of attention the participants are paying to the meeting.

Findings from educational and neuroscience literature show that one of the benefits of SPEIK is that people pay more attention during meetings when the technology is used.[2] Simply by using the technology, the meeting organizer is already combating people's general tendency, in meetings, to lose focus.

Polling makes each person feel as though he or she has a perspective that is considered important.

Typically, people will feel more connected to a collective process if they feel like their participation makes a difference to what happens. By its very nature, audience polling accomplishes this.

The display of polling results focuses participants' attention not just on their own submission, but also on the results obtained from the group.

Many people arrive at meetings with strongly held perspectives about whatever issues are confronting the group. Others may not have strong feelings. By focusing attention on the diversity in the group's perspectives, a message is sent from the polling facilitator—

with the implicit support of the meeting sponsor—that the group's diverse responses on this question are worthy of attention, and perhaps are more important than their individual perspectives.

When results are displayed to the whole group, everyone has access to objective data about the diversity of the group.

In addition to conveying the group's diversity of perspectives, the display of polling results clarifies aspects of this diversity. Hence, it becomes more difficult for assertive voices, experts, or leaders to propagate beliefs they may sincerely have about the groups' diversity that may not be true.

Karen Green
Vice President of Finance, Chair of Diversity Council
AmerisourceBergen Corporation

Ms. Green attended a conference where SPEIK was the core experience of a plenary session for a two-day national conference.

It is really powerful for what this can do in our training. Very powerful. It was neat to see the answers immediately, and to see how this is how I feel, and this is how everyone in the group feels. We stayed excited and were waiting to see what was going to happen next. Energy stayed high the whole time. It made learning fun.

SPEIK can push
participants to have a
more reflective attitude.

One final impact of SPEIK on meetings using the technology is that it often nudges people to be more thoughtful and reflective about their own perspectives. In other words, a well-designed polling process often has the effect of pushing participants toward a more empathetic engagement of different points of view.

The degree to which SPEIK pushes people in a group to become more reflective and considerate of other points of view is a function of many variables. These include the portion of the group's members who tend to be thoughtful and reflective, the atmosphere of the meeting, the skill of the person who crafted the questions, and the person who is facilitating the polling.

Julie Nelson
Senior Fellow, Haas Institute for Diversity and Inclusion,
University of California, Berkeley

Ms. Nelson had deployed SPEIK technology at conferences focused on racial equity.

The value of using the devices was that we had intentionally wanted to engage as many people as possible and when you're having a lot of people in a room, it's really easy for a few voices to dominate. The hand-held voting devices let people see themselves within a larger context.

2.9   **On behalf of a non-profit focused on peace building, we facilitated a three-hour meeting at lunchtime in the middle of the week around issues of trust building as a means of improving life in the metropolitan area.** Initial demographic polling showed that there was a wide diversity of income levels in the room. After the first polling question but before the small group dialogue began, one woman commented that she learned a great deal from the polling process—specifically, that more than 30 percent of the attendees made over $100,000 per year. She herself was from the least affluent category, with household incomes less than $25,000 per year. She admitted that before the meeting, she did not think that people she considered rich would care enough about the community to take time out for such a meeting. She further stated that she had not previously realized how much prejudice she harbored against people in that income category.

Brian Biery
Director of Community Organizing
Flintridge Center, Pasadena, California

Mr. Biery persuaded his organization to invest in SPEIK technology after seeing the authors conduct public meetings with polling devices.

What made you want to pick up audience polling devices for your organization?

There were several community meetings I attended, in part through the Western Justice Center, where the technology was utilized; in particular there was one with youth where I thought it was fascinating to observe, not only the responses in and of themselves, of course, but also the participation level. The engagement was very strong. And with teens it's really complicated because they're thinking about a million different things anyway and there was still a little bit of fooling around and playing around. But for the most part the technology engaged them, the technology enabled them to feel as though they had a voice. The technology enabled the coordinators to be able to acquire actual real-time data that is actionable and could be used to help plan programs to respond to student needs and to think a little bit more broadly about community health.

But thinking about the technology more broadly, it's a mechanism to expand democracy or democratic notions, democratic perspective, civic participation, civic engagement, people feeling they have a voice when so often these days they feel disenfranchised and shut off. Because of the immediacy—not the intimacy—of the response and to be able to chart immediately how everyone in the room is feeling, I think it's going to capture the imagination of folks and really help them to be more active, more thoughtful and talk more about, especially, local issues.

We cannot say how often a polling process moves a significant portion of people to become more thoughtful. Nevertheless, we offer some examples that illustrate this phenomenon as well as our best thinking about why this happens.

Let's reexamine the polling process itself to see why well-crafted and facilitated questions push some participants to become more reflective and thoughtful as indicated in example 2.9.

Initially, polling questions turn participants' attention to their own points of view, which they are forced to define (at least temporarily) while using SPEIK. People are naturally curious about how they compare to others[3], and they are provided with immediate feedback about where they fit within the diversity of the group. In addition, the projected display of the summary of responses suggests that the diversity thereof is worthy of everyone's attention. In most cases, the polling facilitator can affirmatively reinforce the idea that the diversity of perspectives is both positive and also interesting. This can be done with a light touch, such as adding a comment when the collective results are displayed such as, "People have many different views about our core challenges (or whatever). Hmmm....very interesting."

Our sense is that in many instances, it is useful to start the use of SPEIK with questions that include four major question types, which comprise identity, experience, knowledge, and opinion. (The question types will be explained in more depth in the next chapter.) Even if you only ask a few questions each of which seem reasonably relevant to the setting, many people will naturally wonder how answers are related to the topic of the meeting, as well as how answers to different questions might be related to each other. Among participants, there will be varying degrees of curiosity on what could be considered a core question that affects the group: what accounts for the diversity of perspectives in this room?

The shift toward reflective thinking—from a focus on one's own opinion to a curiosity about what is behind one's own and others' opinions—has been considered by some scholars to be a key factor in maximizing the learning that can happen from group interactions. Experts in education and in-group process often use terms like "dialogic attitude" to describe the mindset that involves people becoming more curious about others' opinions and the questioning of their own perspective.[4] Some of the characteristics of a dialogic attitude are:[5]

CHARACTERISTICS OF A DIALOGIC ATTITUDE:

Appreciation of the diversity of perspectives present.

Recognition of the potential relationship between experiences and opinions.

Curiosity about the reasons people have different perspectives.

Openness to exploring how other views might enhance one's own learning.

2.10   **A few years ago, we facilitated a meeting of non-profit and business leaders who had completed a nine-month leadership course.** Their learning goal was to acquire skills related to being servant/leaders for diverse urban populations. Several demographic questions were asked, with each result shown in comparison to census data from the city. The group was quite proud to get statistical confirmation of what they knew from looking around—that the racial composition of the leaders was very close to the city's population. The demographic polling also probed household income, and the results in the room were contrasted with census data. The leaders were dramatically more affluent than the city's population. This was troubling to many participants. An extensive conversation ensued that focused on the potential implications of this finding. Eight months later, members of the group told us that this finding stuck with them as much as anything in the course, and they had come back to it during many subsequent sessions.

The information in example 2.10 had a strong impact on the group because it pushed them to consider something they had not previously considered: that their average income level might have a significant impact on their capacity to serve as leaders of low- to middle-income populations. In essence, seeing how their demographic diversity compared to the community made them ask a number of reflective questions about their leadership:

REFLECTIVE QUESTIONS:
How might our status as income elites affect how we define the city's challenges?
How might our background affect how we define good leadership?
To what extent might we see these issues differently than those with other backgrounds?
How might the differences between the community's personal backgrounds and views and our own affect how they might perceive us?

In the earlier example (2.9), the polling data pushed the low-income woman to examine her prejudice about how much high-income people care about the community. She then began to ask herself some reflective questions: How might my prejudices affect my ability to work cooperatively with others? How might my attitude toward them have an impact on my effectiveness? This is similar to what happened in the later example (2.10)—the polling data and what it said about the similarities and differences and the leaders' relationship to the larger community pushed the group to consider similar reflective questions: Who are we and what are the challenges facing us as a group?

While we would not have predicted either of these results, they were not accidents. Our question-design approach is intended to help groups explore potential linkages between who they are, what they know, what they have experienced, and what they think. In addition, it is important to remember that reflective thinking varies tremendously between groups and among the people in particular groups. A meeting organizer's primary obligation is to create a polling experience that works in the room, and if possible, to provide useful information for the sponsor who is paying for the meeting. Nevertheless, it is often possible to consciously design the polling experience so that it pushes participants to a deeper level of thinking about the circumstances that they each face and that they confront as a group. To this extent, a well designed and executed polling sequence pushes many participants toward thinking of their situation as part of a larger system of entities, behaviors, and beliefs that are interrelated.

For example, there are cases when it is not appropriate to consciously try to design a polling process so that it fosters a dialogic attitude. In the real estate example mentioned earlier (2.5), it would have been wrong-headed to design polling questions with the intention of fostering deep reflection among the attendees present. By contrast, there are cases where you can design SPEIK questions based on what results might be and, if your hunches turn out to be accurate, you can foster a much deeper level of reflection among participants than might otherwise be possible.

2.11   In 2007, we facilitated a meeting in Detroit that was described as the Race Summit; the three-day meeting included more than 200 community leaders, including the mayor, a suburban county executive, and the local Catholic Archbishop. On the first night, we introduced the polling devices with some demographic questions (such as age, income, race, and neighborhood) as well as some experience and opinion questions on various race-related topics such as experiences and perceptions around white flight, economic deterioration of the urban core, community safety, and relations with the police. There was substantial diversity on most of these questions.

At one point, we showed how the responses to some questions were related to the answers to other questions. (The ability to do cross-tabulation will be discussed in chapter 3). One of these showed that the African-American members of the crowd perceived their residential neighborhoods as being much more dangerous than did white participants. This was followed by another cross-tabulation showing that the blacks in the group also viewed the police with much more skepticism and less trust than did the white participants. A very striking hush came over the crowd when the facilitator paused to let the implications of this data sink in—that the black members of the audience, in general, felt less safe in their neighborhoods and more left on their own to handle community safety concerns since they generally did not perceive the police as fundamentally working on their behalf. Through the course of the next two days, several white participants made comments in workshops that this finding was disturbing to them, and helped them see that there was a large divide in experience between white and black middle class leaders trying to work in alliance in developing concrete volunteer projects.

Note that the learning in 2.11 was not that there was a diversity of perspectives around safety or around perceptions of police. It was very specifically the cross-tabulations that created significant new learning because the participants saw that experiences and perceptions varied by a specific factor—racial background—and that discovery was highly relevant to the topic of the meeting. The decision to include this cross-tabulation was based on a hunch by the design team about what the findings might be.

To be clear, we do not have scientific data to support our experience that a well-designed polling experience often pushes some participants in a gathering to a dialogic attitude. This question needs to be studied by academics. In the meantime, we suggest that people considering augmenting meetings through SPEIK spend some time thinking about whether there are ways to use consciously designed questions that will invite reflective thinking on the part of participants.

> SPEIK can give everyone in a meeting a more powerful sense of accomplishment.

When people enter a meeting, many of them have a vague lingering question about whether what they are about to do will accomplish anything. Similarly, at the end of a meeting, people are sometimes not sure whether the meeting produced any result that was noteworthy. Many times, this uncertainty re-enforces the importance of taking notes at a meeting, since meeting minutes at least provide a record of what took place. Of course, the relationship between what those notes say and what happened at the meeting is a matter of some interpretation. We know more than a few facilitators and activists who recognize this, and who strategically position themselves to be meeting note takers, even though this task can be daunting. Having the power of the figurative pen by authoring notes can give someone substantial influence over the subsequent shared narrative about the meeting.

If SPEIK questions are drafted well and deployed appropriately, the results provide further validation that the meeting was meaningful, since there is tangible data about the answers that the participants provided. Even more powerfully, questions can be purposefully designed to help the group make progress toward greater clarity about what they might want to do going forward. (This could range from a clearer sense of the challenges they face, or about which specific actions they might pursue. Strategies for integrating these questions into the meeting will be discussed in Chapter 4).

By giving concrete information about how the group has advanced its thinking, the deployment of SPEIK at a meeting helps address a very common reason why people are often reluctant to go to or to convene meetings: that they often leave without a sense that the meeting accomplished anything.

Diana Hossack
Conference Planner
Washington, DC

Ms. Hossack has had multiple clients who have integrated SPEIK into a conference to augment plenaries or workshop sessions.

You can use it to get buy-in from a set of people on a set of common issues in an effort to move things forward. It provides an immediacy and answer to the questions: what are our priorities? what do I need to do as an individual to move things forward and what do these organizations need to do? You leave feeling like there is a resolution for the work that you have done. That you have not just talked for a day and nothing will happen. We all walked away with a series of action steps and a real tangible sense of knowing what the room wanted to do. It provided closure. Voting on action steps provides a sense that your time was worth it not only because you gained something but that the process gained something.

Endnotes:
[1] Kaner, et. al., 2007.
[2] Burnstein and Lederman, 2001; d'Inverno et al., 2003; Siau et al., 2006; Slain, Abate, Hidges, 2004.
[3] Burton, 2006; Caldwell, 2007; Draper & Brown, 2004; Hinde and Hunt, 2006; Simpson and Oliver, 2007.
[4] Isaacs, W. 1999; Wegerif, R. 1996.
[5] Bohm, D., 1996; Schirch and Campt, 2007.

Sandusky found herself worried that she was out of touch with the membership. Her speech the day before was a case in point. Although she thought she had targeted the most important concerns facing her members, her subsequent conversations with various distributors had raised considerable doubts. Sandusky hoped her staff's new opinion tracking system would put those concerns to rest in the future.

The Banana Distributors Trade Association's top analyst Leona Hart was leading the tracking initiative and had revealed the full scope of the system to the general membership earlier in the day. Sandusky was a little concerned that Hart's talk had been confusing and overly detailed. She was looking forward to getting some honest feedback in a candid, participatory meeting with her 20-person leadership team on how the proposed program was being received.

Sandusky jumped right in. "Are people excited about the tracking system?", she asked. A few eyes shifted back and forth and a couple of heads nodded slightly. Finally, the BDTA's Vice-President of Member Affairs spoke up. "Some of the folks I talked to were really interested," he said. "Yeah," echoed the legal counsel. No one else spoke.

"Any concerns?", Sandusky asked. Again there was a pause and several team members began scrutinizing their notes from the meetings with the distributors. No one said anything.

"Did the distributors understand they would need to be entering data on a weekly basis?", asked Sandusky. Ms. Hart, the analyst who had introduced the program at the meeting spoke up. "Oh I'm sure they got that from my talk," she said. "I was pretty clear about how the software allowed for real time tracking of opinion movements through the revised coding package and statistical tool set." A few folks nodded; a few shared silent glances of mutual confusion.

"Okay," said Sandusky, "and no complaints that the funding for the program is coming out of the banana marketing campaign, eh! That is great! I was really worried about that given how successful the campaign has been. All right then. Let's move on."

An alternative to consider:

How might the meeting with the leadership team been affected if at various points in the meeting, the chief of staff polled the leadership anonymously to assess their opinion about one or more of these questions:

What was their estimate of how well the morning's audience had understood the explanation of the new tracking systems the analyst had earlier explained?

and/or:

What was their level of support for the idea that the opinion tracking system would provide some advantages for the association?

and/or:

What was their assessment of how the membership in general felt about the importance of the tracking system?

and/or:

How much they felt they had made the needed adjustment so they could succeed in the new regulatory and competitive environment they faced?

3.

SPEIK ELEMENTS: QUESTIONS AND ASSOCIATED TOOLS

3

Elements

Now that we have discussed how SPEIK affects meeting stakeholders and modes, it is time to briefly describe the types of questions that are typically asked when using SPEIK systems. We will also discuss some important additional capabilities that are beyond the basic capacity of asking a multiple-choice question that allows one response. These other capabilities are often very important in helping participants and presenters learn more and feel connected to the task at hand.

FIVE TYPES OF QUESTIONS

There are five primary types of keypad questions, each of which lets the group see a different aspect of diversity that exists within it.

- Demographic questions, which reveal diversity in participants' social identities,
- Experience questions, which reveal diversity in what participants have done or been through,
- Fact questions, which reveal diversity in what the participants think they know,
- Opinion or perspective questions, which reveal diversity in participants' viewpoints, and
- Process questions, which reveal diversity in what the group thinks should happen in the meeting.

Let's explore each of these briefly, in turn.

One way to think about demographic questions is that they cover some aspect of each person and his or her internal sense of identity or how he or she is sometimes viewed by other people. These questions also cover the kinds of topic that might come up on a census form which explores characteristics such as age, gender, race/ethnicity, where the participant lives, his or her income, among others.

Some aspects of diversity in identity are addressed in demographic questions. The questions might touch upon obvious characteristics such as age or gender. Some highlight qualities that might not necessarily be guessed correctly; two examples are ethnicity/race or education level. Finally, there are some aspects of demographic diversity that are always invisible, like sexual orientation or zip code of residence.

In most group settings—especially ones in which people do not know each other—there is a natural tendency to wonder how many people in the room share a similar sense of identity. These questions can address this curiosity. These questions also help the group see that there are a variety of responses on whatever dimensions are polled.

**" ...both demographic
and experience
questions help
people increase their
sense of connection."**

While there is no hard distinction between demographic and experience questions, the latter often focus on aspects of participants' makeup that reflect their walk through life and that may not be a part of their permanent identity. There are some experience questions that also refer to things participants did not choose to do but are also things that a census taker would ask. Experience questions can focus on what might be called "episodic" life events, in that they probe whether participants have ever gone through a particular circumstance; alternatively, some experience questions could be thought of as "lifestyle" questions that ask about an ongoing activity in the lives of audience members.

EXPERIENCE QUESTION EXAMPLES:

Have you ever been unwillingly unemployed for more than two weeks?
Have you ever had a friend who you later found out was gay?
How many times per week do you use public transportation?
Which of these activities do you participate in most frequently after you leave your office?

Examples of experience questions:

With experience questions, people have a sense of one another's similarities and, depending on what is asked, participants' shared proclivities may also be revealed. Both demographic and experience questions can be very useful in helping people increase their sense of inter-connectedness. These questions also help a group appreciate the set of experiences that are at play in the room.

> ## FACT QUESTIONS
> ### REVEALING DIVERSITY IN WHAT
> ### THE PARTICIPANTS KNOW

Fact questions probe the extent to which a group of participants has a correct understanding of a fact or concept. Of course, this happens at a specific moment in time, which means that a presenter can ask a fact question at different times during a gathering, and see if there are changes in people's understanding of key facts or concepts. This capacity to show an increase in learning is one of the primary reasons that keypads are used more frequently in the classroom, and why they have a great deal of potential in training settings for adults.

There is good research showing that people are more likely to remember information that is presented to them if polling is integrated as part of the presentation.[1] In addition, fact questions give hard data to presenters or facilitators about what the audience knows or does not know. Our experience has shown us that fact questions can have the effect of opening participants' minds to learning because such questions provide evidence that people individually and/or collectively know less than one thinks.

OPINION QUESTIONS
REVEALING THE DIVERSITY IN WHAT THE PARTICIPANTS THINK

As the name implies, opinion questions probe participants' assessment of some thing, event, or situation. Clearly, the range of questions here varies tremendously, and can be as serious as "How much does sexual assault undermine military morale compared to other challenges?", or as lighthearted as "Which of these movie stars would be best to play the birthday girl if a movie was made of her life?"

According to Carcasson[2], there are a few subtypes of opinion questions that bear additional definition. Prioritization questions ask participants to express the order of importance of a list of problems, values, actions, and so on. Assessment questions ask participants to give feedback on the gathering in which they have been involved. (We will briefly discuss the use of polling in evaluating a gathering in this chapter.)

In general, interactive polling questions help bring some clarity and specificity about what people agree and disagree about related to their shared interest. If the goal of the meeting is to help a group move forward, it is extremely useful to know the degree to which the group has a shared sense of values, problem analyses, or preferred actions. Sometimes, opinion questions help clarify a group's readiness to move together sooner than group leaders might have expected. But things can go the other way too, and opinion questions can help a group discover that there are underlying differences that need to be worked through during the meeting.

Process questions are a specific type of opinion question. These questions give the group a chance to weigh in on what has happened or will happen in the course of the meeting. Process questions might range from matters like personal comfort (Which way, if any, should the temperature in this hall be adjusted?) to issues that impact the agenda of the meeting. (Which of the four remaining agenda items should be eliminated if we run short on time?)

SPEIK FEATURES THAT SIGNIFICANTLY AUGMENT QUESTIONS

There are some capacities of SPEIK systems that go beyond the basic display of a summary response to a multiple-choice question.

Multiple Responses

In many cases, the most appropriate way to pose a question is to only allow one response. However, there are many cases in which having only one choice would make people feel limited as they answered the question. Many SPEIK systems allow the programming of questions that have more than one response, and in some cases are able to give different weights to the multiple responses that are submitted. The prioritization questions mentioned above usually use this feature.

Anonymity

Many meeting strategists find the anonymity of the participants' responses to be a key advantage because of the candor that is fostered. This is how that anonymity occurs for polling systems in which the devices are handed out: The SPEIK system tracks all responses from each device. During polling, the system is keeping a record of how each device responded to every question, resulting in a complete database when polling closes. If the devices were distributed without a record being kept of which person had which device, each individual can feel confident that no one can ever know how they answered the questions. In cases when anonymity is not desired, the devices can be assigned to individuals, and the final polling database has a record of all of their votes.

Displaying External Data To Help Participants See The Bigger Picture

The display of polling results helps a group get more clarity about the diversity of its demographics, experiences, factual knowledge, and opinions. Sometimes, it is powerful to see how these aspects of the group compare to a relevant population outside of the room. Certain keypad systems allow this comparison to be done quickly, and in a way that is easy to digest.

To understand the possible value of this feature, imagine a community meeting in a gentrifying area. It would likely be useful to ask an age demographic question. Imagine that at such a meeting, this question demonstrated that more than a third of the participants were under 35, and more than a third were over 65. This would certainly be a notable result on its own, but perhaps might generate more insight if the display of the results was supplemented by a graphic showing how the neighborhood's age demographic compared to the city-wide population that, for instance, might not be as skewed to either end of the age spectrum. (See figure 1 for an example.)

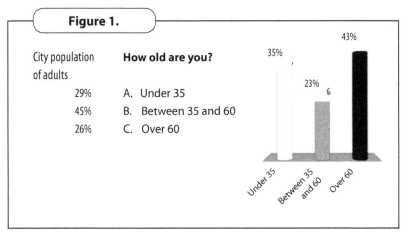

Figure 1.

City population of adults

How old are you?

29%	A. Under 35
45%	B. Between 35 and 60
26%	C. Over 60

35% 23% 43%

Under 35 Between 35 and 60 Over 60

Cross Tabulations

Many SPEIK systems allow a computer to display a graph that will show how the answers to one question can be interpreted in light of the answers to another question. Most statisticians call such a display a cross-tabulation, or cross-tab for short.

Cross-tabs are particularly useful in helping a group generate important insights that might help it improve its collective thinking. They encourage people to begin considering how their demographics, experiences, and opinions might be related to each other in ways they may not have previously considered. Let's return to the hypothetical example of the community meeting in a gentrifying neighborhood. To the example, add the additional wrinkle that the city council is considering modifications to its rent stabilization regime. In a neighborhood meeting to help refine community issues, it might make sense to include a demographic question about whether the group participants rent or own their home.

The answer to this question would undoubtedly be useful. Now imagine that the meeting organizer runs a cross-tab to show how the age question relates to the rent/own question. It could very well be that the large majority of seniors are long-term renters, and a smaller portion of seniors own property, while the lion's share of people under 35 own, and the smaller portion rent. (See figure 2.) Or this might cut the opposite way, with seniors being more likely to own and young people more likely to rent. (See figure 3). Even though

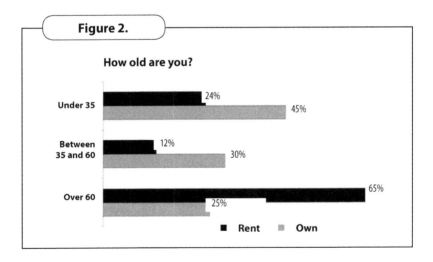

Figure 2.

How old are you?

- Under 35: Rent 24%, Own 45%
- Between 35 and 60: Rent 12%, Own 30%
- Over 60: Rent 65%, Own 25%

■ Rent ▨ Own

renters and owners and seniors and young people have overlapping interests, each of these groups also has divergent interests. Having the cross-tab information would likely help the meeting presenter and the participants engage in a much more focused discussion depending on the underlying realities of the group's demographics and experiences.

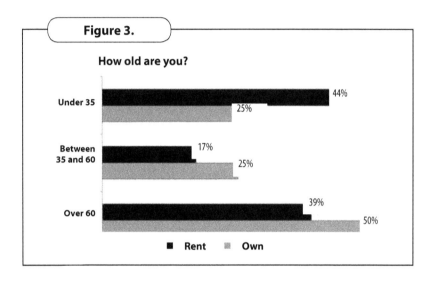

John Brothers
Board Chair
Alliance for Non-profit Management

Mr. Brothers attended a conference plenary session where his membership used SPEIK as part of a member survey.

In my consulting firm, we have used an on-line version of the technology. As the Alliance, we have been struggling to get good data on the needs of our members. I thought that the cross-tabs were the most valuable, and we have never done anything like that. People in our organization are always saying, "Our members want this." But we have never been able to say these kinds of members feel like this, these kinds of members feel like that. Knowing the different subgroups will allow us to tailor our services to our members more effectively.

Group Competitions

An additional tool that some SPEIK systems provide is the ability to conduct competitions using the keypads. In such a competition, the group is asked a fact question, and groups can compete by seeing which group has the highest percentage of people who answer the question correctly, or which group gave the fastest correct answers.

It is remarkable how energizing a short–term competition can be to a gathering if questions are well crafted. The teams can be based on something rather random like birth season, section of room, odd or even numbered table, or on real differences in the room, such as age, gender, or neighborhood. Even though people know that there will not be a prize, their desire to win the competition is often very high, resulting in a stimulating atmosphere that helps create an enjoyable meeting. In large meetings, we have sometimes used competitions to provide participants with a well-needed respite from the regular program agenda.

Donna Sharp
Senior Trainer
Sodexho USA

Ms. Sharp saw her first SPEIK demonstration in 2011.

It is a great tool. We are trying different ways of keeping people engaged and a lot of time we tend to lose them to the cell phone and their devices. It helps to clear up some misinformation, since many things we thought were right, were in fact wrong. I love the competition too! At the end of it, you had to say, if I am wrong, maybe the other person is wrong, we can open up a dialogue to find out the real answer.

USING AUDIENCE INTERACTIVITY IN DIFFERENT PHASES OF THE GATHERING

Theories abound about what a gathering is and how we might most effectively model it. In order to initially talk about SPEIK in a general way that applies to all gatherings, we are going to use a very simple common framework for different types of gatherings. The model progresses chronologically from 1) Orientation—getting people focused and ready for the meeting, 2) Core Content—the primary activity of the gathering, and 3) Closure—whatever is done to signal the end of the experience, including potentially evaluating it.

Table 1 shows how this simple framework relates to different parts of meetings including speeches, trainings, workshops, and conferences.

Table 1.

	Orientation	Core content	Closure
Speech/ Training/ Panel Discussion	Opening joke Acknowledgments	Speech Training content Panel discussion Audience Q&A	Charge to audience Compelling quote
Conference	Welcome remarks Opening keynote	Sessions	Closing keynote Evaluation
Facilitated workshop	Introduction Initial check-in	Group discussions in various formats	Evaluation Closing remarks Final ritual

Getting people ready for a meeting is a critical task; whether it is for the first three minutes of a short speech or the first half day of a week-long retreat, meeting organizers/presenters usually spend some energy on helping the participants feel reasonably grounded in the setting they are in. In putting together an orientation for the participants, the organizer/presenter aspires to create an experience that would nudge participants to have positive answers to a few questions that are likely lingering in their minds at the start of a gathering.

EXAMPLE QUESTIONS:

To what extent is this setting one that I can comfortably be in for the duration of this gathering?

How am I connected to the primary content that are the central issues here?

How am I connected to the other people, whether audience members or the meeting organizers?

In this initial phase of a gathering, the meeting presenter, who may have been planning the event for some time, often asks him or herself: Are there any adjustments we can make in light of who actually showed up in contrast to whom we thought would show up? SPEIK can help presenters find out the composition of the audience in whatever ways they think are useful so that the content or process can best be tailored to specific participant needs.

Polling questions for the orientation part of the gathering can be designed to provide answers to these questions—questions that tend to encourage more energized engagement of participants and presenters. Though using SPEIK in the early part of a meeting potentially helps presenters make adjustments, the larger value of polling concerns the impact on the audience. With reasonably savvy design, SPEIK helps in a number of ways, specifically by:

Establishing a participatory element of the meeting

Interactive polling early in the orientation in the gathering tells each participant that in this meeting, every person's voice matters.

Helping people discover mutual traits

By asking a mix of demographic, experience, and opinion questions, using SPEIK in an orientation phase often helps people not only know that they are accepted for who they are, but also that there are a number of people in the room with whom they may feel certain similarities.

Setting the emotional tone

If done skillfully, the way that SPEIK questions are presented can embrace a spirit of fun and discovery that can help the rest of the gathering, even if the core topic is serious or difficult.

Positioning the gathering as a chance for learning

By showing that many people may be misinformed about some key relevant facts, interactive polls can often enhance the willingness of the group to keep an open mind and see the meeting as a learning opportunity.

Helping a group clarify its task in light of its relationship to others not in the room

The demographics of the gathered group can be shown in comparison to the larger population that it may think it represents. Seeing the level of similarity with the larger population on whose behalf it is acting (if this is relevant) may sharpen the understanding of the task at hand.

Elliott Bronstein
Public Information Officer
Seattle Office for Civil Rights

Mr. Bronstein's office repeatedly used SPEIK to gain public input on a community initiative.

It creates an intimate space out of an impersonal space. Because you've got a hundred people out there—and some are friends and some are not and they may be sitting at different tables—but, because it's so much fun and it's so interesting to do, it winds up creating a bond. It brings people together because—you look at a room of a hundred people, you don't know what they're thinking. Now you do.

USING AUDIENCE POLLING TO HELP WITH THE ORIENTATION PHASE

After each participant has procured a usable polling device, and the preliminaries have been said, at some point it will be time to begin the first sequence of polling questions (different strategies for getting the devices to the participants will be discussed in Appendix 1). From the standpoint of engaging the participants, the first polling question is very important. As of this writing (Spring 2015) many people have not used SPEIK in any setting before. The adage "you never get a second chance to make a first impression" also applies to the technology. We strongly recommend using a warm-up question that is labeled and presented as just that. This warm-up question should be explicitly labeled as such so that the participants know it does not really matter for the purposes of the meeting.

This serves two key purposes. First, it is important to confirm that after all the testing and retesting that you have done, the SPEIK system is actually working (more on testing in Appendix 1). Even though the systems are very reliable, they will sometimes have breakdowns that require attention. While it is not a good thing if the system does not work, it is much better for you and the audience to discover this on a question that is clearly designed as a throwaway.

The warm-up question also serves an important additional purpose—introducing the group to SPEIK and to the pleasant, inclusive, and participatory spirit intended to accompany its use. It also potentially serves as a preview of the entire meeting. Moreover, a warm-up question that generates a positive spirit and brings a smile to a few faces helps install the notion in the participants' brains that "SPEIK = fun." As we will see later, even if the meeting will be on a sad topic—such as the aftermath of a murder—it is still possible to create an appropriate mood-lifting warm-up question.

How To Create A Good Warm Up Question

The three most critical elements of a good warm-up question are, from most to least important, inclusivity, light-heartedness, and topicality.

Inclusivity: the question and the options should be framed so that everyone is likely to see an answer to which they can relate.

The warm-up question should be an experience or opinion question, and should be constructed such that no matter how non-mainstream someone is, each person should see an option that he or she can identify with. Furthermore, the options for answering should be phrased so everyone can be equally proud of their answer. If the meeting is in a football-crazy college town in September, it may be useful to ask about the prospects for the team, but it would be important to include an answer that allows people who do not follow or who dislike football to proudly express themselves.

Light-heartedness: if possible, at least one or two of the answers should bring a smile to a few faces.

If possible, the question and the answers should be at least a slight mood-lifter that will bring a smile to at least a few faces, no matter the distribution of the answers. If possible, some of the answer options should be somewhat humorous, even when initially read before any answers are shown. The reveal of the distribution of answers will allow an opportunity for an additional moment of laughter. Moments of shared levity can be essential to people feeling

like the meeting is a good place for them to be. Such questions also help establish the idea that in this meeting, people are not taking themselves too seriously, and that the diversity of the group's answers can itself be enjoyable to discover.

Topicality: if possible, the subject of the question should refer to something that may be on the minds of the audience.

Interactive polling experiences within a few days of big national events—such as the Oscars, the Super Bowl, or a holiday—sometimes provide an easy way to construct a question that generates a small buzz in the room. Having a warm-up question that is linked to something current also gives the session a sense of vitality and leaves participants with the correct impression that the polling experience has been customized for them. Examples of setting-specific topics would be a fire alarm that caused an evacuation earlier in the day, a recent traffic-impeding blizzard, or the band at a previous night's conference reception that was uncommonly good or awful.

If you attempt to design a warm-up question that is topical, be very careful that you are following the more important inclusivity rule above. Even if everyone you know is talking about the major upset in the national championship basketball game two nights ago, there are likely many people who have not even heard of the game.

Here are a few examples of warm-up questions that illustrate how a question can manifest each of these principles to different extents.

Q. Which comes closest to how well you think our football team will do this year?

1. I have already pre-ordered a "We are the Champions" t-shirt!

2. Playoffs?.... yes. But we're at least one year away.

3. The season will be fair to middlin'

4. The theme song this season should be "Cryin' Time".

5. I have many more important things to think about than over-grown young men in tight pants.

For almost the entire month of February 2009, our warm-up question was constructed by showing the prelude picture slide below, then asking a question:

Q. Remember this hat from Inauguration Day?

This polling question would follow:

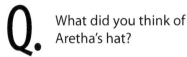

Q. What did you think of
Aretha's hat?

A.

1. It was da bomb!
2. Kinda cool, kinda out there.
3. It must have warmed her head,
   cuz it did not warm my heart.
4. It bombed!

If a warm-up question has been executed well, a few people will have laughed, and many will have smiles on their faces. Most importantly, there should be a feeling of anticipation in the air for more opportunities to participate and glimpse into the diversity of the group.

What Happens After The Warm-Up Question

Besides wondering whether the meeting setting is a comfortable one for them, a nagging question for meeting participants concerns their connection with the other people in the room. After a warm-up question, it is usually a good idea to ask at least a few questions that help the participants know who came to the meeting, assuming they do not know each other well already. We have found that there is a natural tendency for people to want to know how many people are like them at the meeting. The goal is to develop a set of questions that satisfies this curiosity and at the same time supports whatever goals the sponsor might have for the meeting. These questions may also push participants to think more deeply about the diversity in the group.

The number of keypad questions that can be asked before a significant portion of people tire of responding varies greatly, depending on the purpose and duration of the meeting, the audience, the topic, and more importantly, audience perceptions about the meeting sponsor. For the sake of this discussion, let us assume that there are about six minutes of flexibility in the agenda, which would roughly be about eight to nine questions after the warm-up question. How should this sequence of questions be constructed?

When designing an initial set of "Who is Here?" questions, we suggest that the following four issues be kept in mind.

FOUR ISSUES FOR "WHO IS HERE" QUESTIONS:

1. What question(s) will allow the participants to reveal some part of their identity, experience, or opinion that will, in this particular setting, help them feel acknowledged, or will be perceived as relevant to the topic of the meeting?

2. Assuming that the meeting participants were not mandated to be there, what question(s) will allow the presenter to positively comment on the diversity in the room, and take note of relevant sub-groups that might be strongly or weakly represented?

3. What question(s) will likely generate interest or curiosity among the more thoughtful of those present about how identities, experiences, knowledge, and opinions might affect each other?

4. What question(s) will be useful to meeting sponsors because they will focus on aspects of diversity (especially in experience or opinion) that may be useful in the post-meeting analysis of the polling questions?

We have generally found that it is usually best that the initial "who is here" set of questions include demographic questions, experience questions, and opinion questions—typically in that order. Depending on the type of meeting, sometimes fact questions during the orientation phase of the gathering can also be helpful.

People are used to answering some basic identity questions (such as age), so asking a few arguably relevant questions in this vein satisfies curiosity while not being off-putting.

Demographic questions allow people to declare their membership in an identity group. The trick is to choose aspects of identity around which there is diversity, and that are plausibly relevant to the meeting. This kind of question is particularly relevant when participants have exercised a great deal of discretion in their choice to attend the meeting. Demographic questions let the group see who elected to be there, and potentially allow the facilitator to create a moment of group self-congratulation. For instance, at community meetings, we have shouted out "Girl Power" on many occasions when women were more than 55 percent of a room, but we were ready to say "Let's hear it for the boys!" if the numbers were flipped. On the other hand, there are settings in which is it very important to remind the entire group about subpopulations that may be underrepresented. This is particularly true at community meetings that are attempting to probe a public response to an issue.

But even at meetings that are not completely voluntary—such as corporate meetings—demographic questions can still be helpful. For example, imagine a two-day meeting of a division of a pharmaceutical company that is intended to include people from the marketing, sales, and research departments. Even though the conference is mostly required, there might be an over- or under-representation from the different departments at a plenary session, and this might happen for a variety of reasons. If the meeting was intended to expose employees to a new strategy developed by senior management, it might be very useful to the meeting to know if there are groups who were not proportionately represented.

No matter what type of meeting, it is generally not helpful to criticize groups for being over- or under-represented. But it can often be useful to remind everyone gathered to consider the perspective of sub-groups that may be disproportionally small at that particular meeting.

In 2007, AmericaSpeaks produced and designed Community Congress II, in which 2,500 people in five different cities gathered to discuss the rebuilding of New Orleans after Hurricane Katrina. About half the participants were in New Orleans; the other half participated via satellite from Atlanta, Baton Rouge, Dallas, and Houston. This meeting was a follow-up to Community Congress I, a meeting with 500 people 10 weeks earlier where 70 percent of attendees had incomes of more than $100,000 per year. A critical success factor for the meeting was engaging a large percentage of people who had pre-Katrina incomes below the poverty line, since 40 percent of the city's below-poverty population had always been grossly underrepresented at key community meetings. When a demographic question was asked about pre-Katrina income, the distribution of answers was displayed, right along with the distribution of incomes in the city before the storm. The fact that 25 percent of those present had incomes below poverty was considered a big victory, and a cheer went up in all five meeting sites. This fact also added to the credibility of the meeting in the minds of the meeting's funders.

We have found it most useful to have the initial "Who is here?" questions to seamlessly transition from demographic questions into a few that focus on people's experiences that are relevant to the meeting. Asking the right set of experience questions helps remind the group that people will have a wide variety of different life events that are related to the core topics of the meeting.

> **"...it is generally not useful to criticize groups for being over- or under-represented."**

Experience questions have the effect of increasing the participants' sense of who is present, but each experience question also reminds them that the backgrounds that they bring to the topic may be only one subset of many different possibilities. In this way, the questions nudge the participants to think about different points of view on the main topic of the meeting. Even if the core content of the meeting is just one speaker telling his or her story, good experience questions can help people become more curious about stories other than their own.

3.2

We were engaged by a new police chief to facilitate some community meetings to help lay the groundwork for a renewed community-policing strategy. During the meetings, we asked an early polling question that explored people's experience with the police department. The options included: having had the police respond after being victimized by a crime, having been arrested for infractions they had committed, and having felt unfairly harassed by police officers.

SPEIK questions about such experiences help the group feel connected to itself in that everyone sees tangible evidence of common experiences the group has that it might not otherwise understand. Of course, the questions should be designed to give further insight about the connection between people, and not tell people what they already know by the nature of the meeting.

In many cases, it is sensible to go directly from a few well-designed demographic and experience questions to the core content of the meeting. However, it is often valuable to ask a few opinion questions so that everyone knows where they initially stand on aspects of the core content that is about to follow. This is particularly true during meetings that are centered on obtaining feedback or fostering crosstalk by the participants.

3.3

A few years ago, we conducted a series of dialogues about the problems facing young people from poor communities, and the challenges to youth taking better control over their circumstances. Most of the meetings were in detention facilities, but a few were in communities. In the community based meetings, we asked one question about whether people had been incarcerated or not, and a second one about the length of time in incarceration. In the meetings in detention facilities, there was no need to ask whether or not they had been incarcerated. In both meetings, we asked about whether the youth had family members who had been victims of crimes. We were subsequently told by detention staff supervisors that it was useful for their staff and participants to think about the way in which the youth had been crime victims as well as perpetrators.

"...good experience questions can help people become more curious about stories other than their own."

Getting an initial read on the variety of opinions on the subject of the meeting is often helpful in creating anticipatory excitement about the gathering. The key design task is to frame questions that highlight diversity of opinions—that is, disagreement—and to do so in a way that furthers the purpose of the meeting. Essentially, there are times when highlighting the diversity of opinion early in a meeting is helpful, and there are times when emphasizing disagreements during the orientation phase is counter-productive.

For instance, the meeting may have been called partially because there is an unresolved disagreement about the nature or scope of a problem, and this lingering disagreement is undermining the ability of the group to move forward. In such a case, there may be significant advantages to making the diversity of opinion public early in the meeting.

3.4

Our client was a Fortune 500 company having a national meeting of about 50 middle managers. The purpose of the meeting was to create more effective relationships between these geographically dispersed managers and to increase their collective understanding about how to cooperate in a way that sparked more innovation. Our responsibility was not to manage the entire all-day meeting, but only to conduct a community-building initial SPEIK experience.

In addition to asking a number of demographic and experience questions to create a sense of community, we also asked some opinion questions about how the group rated the company's morale and their tendency to innovate compared to competitors. We were later told by the client that the polling session accelerated the ability of the group to have a candid discussion about the weaknesses in the company's internal culture.

Conversely, as noted above, there are times when unearthing underlying disagreements around controversial topics early in the meeting is actually unhealthy, and will more likely worsen the tone of the meeting.

3.5

Before the meeting about rebuilding New Orleans after Hurricane Katrina, AmericaSpeaks convened focus groups to help refine small group discussion questions and SPEIK questions. The meeting design team had already decided that the meeting would be framed as an opportunity to create a renewed New Orleans that was more inclusive of all groups. When probed about the possibility of bringing up racial divisions that existed in the city before the storm, both white and black participants strongly urged us to avoid raising any racial issues explicitly, out of a fear that raising this topic would cause enough tension as to significantly harm the meeting.

It is important to use good judgment in sorting out whether bringing up a controversial issue with the transparency of SPEIK is likely to be helpful to the goals of the meeting.

There are two reasons to ask fact questions in an orientation phase. First, asking fact questions brings a high level of attention to the topic at hand. A polling question makes people much more likely to remember a fact than if it is simply mentioned. Second, fact questions can open people's minds for learning. The most powerful fact questions are ones that are highly relevant and about which many people are misinformed. This allows the polling facilitator to create a moment that alerts the group that it knows less than it should about something that is important. If a substantial portion of the participants asserts an incorrect answer, they get direct—but non-embarrassing—feedback that there is at least one important gap in their knowledge. Moreover, when the entire group sees that a large portion of the participants is not aware of a relevant fact, people who have given correct and incorrect answers are both reminded that the group's collective knowledge can be imperfect. This reminder often helps foster a sense of humility that is useful for on-going learning.

Generally, fact questions are most likely to be useful before a speech or training that is intended to convey information (as in a primarily download session), and generally least likely to be helpful before a facilitated session whose purpose is to create understanding and collaboration among participants. When considering using a fact question during orientation, a major factor is the relevance of that fact to the core communications mode of the meeting. But there are some additional factors to consider, as follows.

"…the most powerful fact questions are ones that are highly relevant and about which many people are misinformed."

1. Does the question highlight a fact or concept that a reasonable portion of the group would find at least moderately interesting?

2. Has a set of answer options been created that test relevant knowledge? The answer options should be designed to be broad enough so that the differences are not trivial, but narrow enough so that all the answers are plausible. Imagine, for example, a company-wide biennial planning meeting for a medical device manufacturer. During an orientation session, it might be useful to make sure attendees contextualize the meeting in light of the company's recent success in the marketplace. In an interactive opening session, one way of doing this might be to ask a fact question about how much the total market for medical devices had grown in the previous year. It would probably not be useful to include an answer of 40 percent, since this would be virtually inconceivable. At the same time, having all of the answers range from 8.2 percent to 10.2 percent would arguably turn the question from an exercise in which people were testing their relevant knowledge into a mere trivia game.

3. The entire set of questions during orientation—and how the polling facilitator comments upon the answers—can invite the participants to see the group afresh and to see its challenges from a variety of points of view. Some people will accept this invitation, and in doing so cause the shift toward a more reflective mindset.

"...fact questions can open people's minds for learning."

Jenn Lammers
National Program Director
Alliance for Non-profit Management

Ms. Lammers used SPEIK to conduct a member survey at her annual national conference in 2014.

The technology was a great way to have everybody in the room fully participate, to feel heard, and be counted. I was really impressed by how many people said that they really spoke their piece in the session. It really set a great tone for the rest of the conference. This is a great tool to have if you are a convener or an event planner. Had I seen it beforehand, I might have thought differently—like the game playing and the way it creates camaraderie, or the use of personal questions. You think you know how you are going to use it from hearing about it, but you think of different things when you see it.

PHASE 2:
CORE CONTENT

If done successfully, the orientation will have put people in a receptive mood. Still, people can always disengage from the meeting, either by physically leaving or by mentally checking out. The ability to hold the attention of the participant is, of course, primarily a function of the quality of the agenda and the skill of the presenter(s). SPEIK systems can help with the problems of disengagement because of the following effects they have on the gathering:

Revealing Perspectives That Are Often Repressed

The anonymity of the polling devices allows people to express—and meeting presenters to know about—relevant perspectives that may be unpopular and hard to express openly.

Signaling Areas For Possible Adjustments of the Gathering

Presenters can use the information about what participants are learning and thinking—including the degree of consensus and dissent—to make appropriate modifications in the content or processes being used.

Shifting the Mood

As we have conveyed already, the primary way that SPEIK works is by shifting the focus of the thoughts of each participant back and forth between individual and group, and doing so in a way that serves the meeting's goals. Sometimes, what the group also needs is a shift from relatively light topics to more serious ones, or from heavy topics to ones that are lighter in tone. SPEIK can be very useful in these circumstances. Of course, as experienced meeting professionals, we feel compelled to add that coming up with strategies to shift a group's mood is a relatively advanced group management skill.

Letting the Group Know That It Has Power Over Its Own Experience

In the middle of a gathering, interactivity can allow a group to give feedback to the meeting organizer about how well the meeting is fulfilling its needs in a way that potentially allows for some adjustments to be made.

Designing polling questions that integrate with core content is very challenging and requires extensive planning and skillful execution. Presenters need to be mindful that the task of integrating polling questions is a different task when it comes to speeches, conferences, and facilitated sessions. (The differences are explored in Chapter 4).

There are two ways to orient questions that augment participants' relationship to the core content of the meeting. One is to pose *content questions* that reveal participant experiences, knowledge, or opinions as related to the topic. The other is to pose *process questions* that obtain the perspectives of the participants on the actual process of the meeting they are experiencing; these questions would most likely be framed as opinion questions, though there might be times when framing them as experience questions is also useful. Making agenda adjustments based on polling results not only creates more fine-tuned experiences, but a presenter who makes observable adjustments is more likely to be perceived as being very responsive to the group.

Content Modifications to Suit the Audience

When a content question is asked, the presenter can get a strong sense of how the group is relating to the material being delivered, and potentially make some adjustments based on that information. Making such adjustments, especially if the presenter conveys that he or she is doing so, increases the sense among the participants that the meeting and the presenter are being responsive to them. The following are some examples of questions in the core content phases of a speech, a conference, and a workshop that illustrate how the polling allows meeting organizers to make useful adjustments.

QUESTIONS TO ADJUST A SPEECH:

In the middle of a speech on sexual assault in the military, a speaker might pose the following fact question:

Q. What percentage of service people were sexually assaulted last year?

If the number of people who gave correct or almost correct answers is relatively low (say under 20 percent) the speaker might decide to spend a substantial amount of time on issues related to the causes and the impact of people not knowing the prevalence of this problem. If the number of people who know the correct answer is relatively high, the speaker might spontaneously decide to spend some time on insensitivity, but perhaps more time on other issues, such as retaliation against complainants.

At the end of Day 1 of a multi-day conference about volunteerism, the following experience question might be put to the attendees:

Q. How many volunteer hours did you perform last month?

If a large percentage of a meeting's attendees are spending very little time doing volunteer work, the presenter might highlight a session or track the next day about achieving more work/life balance. On the other hand, if a high percentage of attendees spend substantial time doing volunteer work, the presenter might highlight a different session or track, such as one that helps people contemplate the benefits of volunteering.

In a facilitated session designed to help a group of first-line managers improve inter-division communication, a workshop leader might ask this opinion question:

Q. How effective have management's efforts been over the past year to improve morale?

Three possible outcomes of such a question are broad agreement that the strategies have been effective, agreement they have not been effective, and a divergence opinion about whether they have been effective or not. Obviously, a savvy facilitator would respond very differently to each of these three possibilities.

Process Modification to Suit the Audience

One reason integrating SPEIK into the core content of a meeting is challenging is the need to both appear to be and to actually be responsive to the attendees. In many circumstances, a presenter can productively increase a group's sense of its own agency by asking for feedback and making adjustments in the process of the meeting based on the response. The difficulty is that the results of the questions are not known before the question is asked. If a presenter is going to ask a group a process question in the middle of a gathering, it is probably best to be in a position to adapt to the answer.

A speaker who has more material than time might let the group decide whether the bulk of the remaining time was spent in question-and-answer or in delivering prepared materials. For instance, at a natural transition point midway through the allotted time for the speech, a speaker might ask:

> In our remaining time, would you prefer more information about punishment for offenders or more reasons why people offend?

In the middle of a conference, organizers might ask attendees about any adjustments they might like to see in their conference experience. This might look like the following question:

> For our remaining two days, would you like our opening session tomorrow to start earlier and end earlier, stay as it is, or start later and end later?

Sometimes during a facilitated process with medium-sized groups (15 to 50 people) facilitators face a dilemma about whether to have a discussion based on the full group or multiple small groups. If the facilitator felt that each of these might have equal value for the group, he or she might empower the group by asking:

> Q. Should we stay in the plenary session or divide into small groups?

3.6   **At an intensive, 5-weekend training for community change agents, we heard grumblings about the agenda not providing enough flexibility for participants to engage in conversations on difficult subjects like race with each other.** Near the end of one weekend, we offered participants a vote—continue with the written agenda or have a participant-driven dialogue. They overwhelmingly chose to engage in dialogue. As a secondary question, we gave them the choice of a large-group dialogue, with all 25 participants, or in small group dialogues. Again, the choice of the group was clear—they opted for small group dialogues. After a short conversation to choose a topic, they were off in a session of their own design, on a topic of their own choosing, and were consequently deeply engaged in the session they created. Empowering participants to choose how to spend their time at a conference presents a potential of loss of control for the facilitator, but if done well can move groups further towards collective ownership of their conversations.

As a gathering is coming to a close, many people hope that it will be tied up in a way that feels inclusive and coherent. Despite this, we find that meeting organizers often do not pay much attention to people's need for closure. However, many people want to conclude a meeting in a way that feels good. Fortunately, a facilitator using SPEIK can wrap things up positively, even if the meeting organizers made no provision for this. Polling questions can be effective as part of a wrap-up because they can be programmed to:

Check the degree of change in knowledge or perspective.

By asking the same question before and after a meeting, a polling facilitator can know with some precision how much participants' perspectives have changed as a result of the meeting. An alternative strategy for getting the same information is to ask participants to assess how much their knowledge or opinions have changed.

Generate detailed feedback about the gathering.

By collecting answers to questions about the effectiveness of different elements of the gathering, meeting organizers and sponsors can learn which parts worked better than others. The evaluation is already in a computer database, which means meeting organizers do not have to manually input the data before analyzing it. In addition, automated collection of the data means that the post-meeting analysis can determine relatively easily if some sub-groups of participants got more out of the gathering than others.

Clarify preferred or expected next steps.

Polling questions at the end of a meeting can allow a group to clarify its level of support and opposition for specific courses of action. You can ask people about what behavioral changes they expect from individuals or from the group. Whether the group is hopeful or pessimistic about change, you can ask at the next meeting how much change has occurred.

Polling questions can also clarify a group's predictions about what changes in the group are most likely to come about. Such group predictions can serve as an accountability check on groups that meet periodically, since past predictions can be compared to recent progress.

3.7 **National Institutes of Health (NIH) engaged us to augment a meeting of bioethicists with the goal of streamlining the Institutional Review Board (IRB) process.** IRBs review the extent to which studies harm human subjects, but across the country there is little consistency in the outcomes from one institution to the next. The NIH hoped these bioethicists would find consensus on procedures that produced minimal chance of harm to participants. Procedures such as blood draws were considered, and the keypads allowed for a quick vote to see if there was consensus on which procedures could be considered low risk. The meeting was fruitful, not because consensus was reached, but because the NIH quickly understood that there was very little agreement. The ensuing conversations pinpointed vague language in federal standards as the culprit.

Avis Ridley-Thomas
Co-founder
Days of Dialogue, Los Angeles

Ms. Ridley-Thomas has been organizing community dialogues since 1995. The effort began with a focus on race relations.

So about how many Days of Dialogue have you done?

Well, we've done dozens. I haven't counted them but the topics have included things like violence on a particular corridor in Los Angeles and treatment of the mentally ill and certainly recently the killing of Trayvon Martin by a Neighborhood Watch volunteer in Florida, and a police shooting of Michael Brown, and locally the police shooting of a mentally ill young man.

How did you come to be exposed to the idea of audience polling as an enhancement to meetings?

I was exposed to audience polling first through AmericaSpeaks. They partnered with us when I was director of the City Attorney's dispute resolution program. And they trained our mediators to do a statewide dialogue on healthcare under Governor Schwarzenegger. I knew about polling. I didn't train, nor did I participate in that dialogue; I was aware that there was this large-scale communication process going on in the AmericaSpeaks forums. And then, after I retired from the City Attorney's office, Dr. David Campt exposed us close up to audience polling in our Days of Dialogue on the economic crisis and community health in Los Angeles. That was February 2012.

What did you notice about it as a tool for meetings that made you potentially want to start using it?

It absolutely enhanced the experience in so many ways. People simply felt better about what they were doing in

Avis Ridley-Thomas, continued

communicating because they understood more what was happening in the environment, what opinions others had, and what the demographics of the room reflected. It was just a better experience of having meetings and I wanted to incorporate that in every session that we conducted after that initial personal experience.

How has your use of polling changed?

I used them at the beginning and the end. Not in the middle of the dialogue like AmericaSpeaks did, because participants have told us that it interrupts the flow of dialogue. Using it at the end helps because I'm able to get the information immediately about what the experience was like for the participants. They tell me, overwhelmingly, that the experience of the audience polling was helpful to them. I can see if opinions shifted, you know, the self-reporting of opinions being different—even a small bit different—I think is very, very valuable to have.

Anything else you want to add about using the technology?

I think it helps the participants—they see that what happens when you have authentic dialogue is that your opinion might change. I think that's very valuable for them to have. We get information that says that not only did they benefit from the experience, they would participate again and they think that it was worth their time. I think that having more information about what's happening when you're communicating with individuals in a small-group setting is very valuable to have. I expect to use it now in all of the dialogues that we do.

What Has Changed?

Two strategies for trying to assess how much a gathering has changed participants' knowledge or opinions are asking them to assess how much they have changed, or asking the same question before the event and after and notice the difference. The easiest way is to directly ask the participants to rate how their perspectives have changed since the beginning of the meeting. Example questions of this type are:

> **Q.** How much do you think you learned about climate change from the talk today?

> **Q.** To what extent have your frustrations about our division changed in the two days of this conference?

> **Q.** Has the likelihood of your volunteering for our Ward changed as a result of today's summit?

One advantage of this direct approach is that you only have to ask one question for each dimension of change you want to assess. In addition, the shared experience of seeing that many people have changed their perspective in a positive direction can be a momentum boost to the group.

A second way of using polling questions to assess change is to ask before and after questions on the group's factual knowledge or attitudes. This approach actually provides more accurate information than the direct approach; people do not always accurately assess the degree to which their knowledge or opinions have been changed as a result of an experience.

The downside is that to compare "before" and "after" questions means that the same question must be asked twice during the meeting, which is time-consuming. On the one hand, one advantage of this approach is that you can display the before and after results simultaneously, which lets everyone instantly see the degree of change that has occurred if the polling results are displayed. On the other hand, having people repeat questions that they have already experienced may feel like an energy drain, and your intention is to send people away from the gathering energized.

When thinking through whether to assess change by repeating questions or by asking for personal assessments, it is important to consider which strategy is likely to conclude the meeting on a positive note. If you repeat questions and there is in fact a high degree of change, this finding is revitalizing. But when the displayed summary shows the group that there is no change or movement towards the intended direction, the group may find this discouraging.

How Well Did The Meeting Work?

There are many books about how to design evaluation questions, and we will refer the reader to that literature for an extensive discussion of the subtleties.

If all you want to know is the perceived value of the experience, you can simply ask this question to the participants at the end of the gathering. Such a question might look like this:

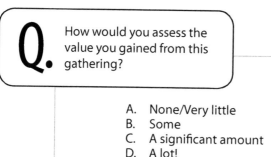

Q. How would you assess the value you gained from this gathering?

A.

A. None/Very little
B. Some
C. A significant amount
D. A lot!

Clearly, you can alter the number of responses to get more or less granularity in the feedback solicited. Generally, we would suggest that questions designed to assess the value of a meeting have no more than six options.

In cases of conferences or extended workshops with multiple elements, it may be useful to get feedback about how much value participants received from each of the components. One important option is to ask multiple questions that poll the group on the value that it received from each element, or to pose one question that asks each participant to specify the one, two, or three components from which they received the most value. One factor to consider in making this choice is the value of the information to future decision-making versus the chance that the participants will experience multiple questions as tedious.

Besides assessing change as discussed, another strategy for making sense of the meeting and for helping the participants do so is to directly ask them about how much value they received from the experience. In constructing such questions, it is important to think through the phrasing of these questions in light of the objectives and the processes of the meeting. For instance, suppose a meeting is a half-day event focused on improving the capacity and motivation of a large sales team. If the event was built around a dynamic motivational speaker and an expert downloading the latest findings from neuroscience about persuasion, the post-event SPEIK questions might focus on motivation and on the value of the information they received. By contrast, suppose the event was designed around discussion in small groups about the personal and organizational obstacles to increased sales. The evaluation questions might ask how the meeting affected the attendees' sense of personal self-awareness and organizational understanding, as well as the value they received from sharing ideas with peers.

As noted, using polling for evaluation has the advantages that the data is already in computer form and that you can potentially perform post-meeting cross-tabs to find out if different groups had different evaluations. Despite these advantages, our opinion is that the most robust evaluations combine multiple choice questions and free-form written feedback. A high or low rating of a meeting or an element in it will not, by itself, convey the reasons why people gave the rating they did. Unless the SPEIK system provides the capacity for written input (and some do), such information can only be obtained from written comments.

Endnotes:
[1] Caldwell, 2007; Carnaghan and Webb, 2007; Horowitz, 2006.
[2] Carcasson and Currie, 2013.

PART 2:
U S E R S
MANUAL

4.
HOW AUDIENCE POLLING CAN AUGMENT SPEECHES, CONFERENCES, AND WORKSHOPS

4

Augment

While interactivity can support presentations, conferences, and facilitated workshops in similar ways, there are also some specific strategies that meeting organizers should use to maximize the benefits of SPEIK for each type of gathering. Within each of these meeting types, there are critical factors that will drive the design task. In this chapter, we will review the key objectives and guidelines for using SPEIK with the three types of meetings, clarify the factors in the meeting that will affect deployment of SPEIK, and include at least one example from our own experience.

USING SPEIK TO IMPROVE SPEECHES, PANEL DISCUSSIONS, AND TRAININGS

As discussed previously, SPEIK can help strengthen the connection between presenters and meeting participants, even when the primary purpose of the interaction is the transmission of ideas in one direction.

The most important variable in making SPEIK effective is the amount of contact between the polling facilitator and the content presenter(s) before the event. The greater amount of communication, the greater the likelihood of close integration of presenter content with keypad questions. Let's divide the amount of contact into three scenarios: 1) minimal contact with speaker, 2) moderate contact, perhaps two to three conversations or email exchanges, and 3) substantial contact, which might include four or more exchanges.

There are several lessons we have learned about the opportunities and challenges of augmenting a download experience such as a speech, panel presentation, or training.

HOW SPEIK CAN HELP:

1. Well-calibrated opinion questions can help a speaker remove unnecessary parts of speeches.

2. Consider having fact questions before opinion questions. Seeing that many people are misinformed about a relevant fact can help the group become less attached to its own opinions in subsequent questions.

3. A polling result that shows the frequency in the room of a relevant experience can help the group connect to a story from the presenter.

4. Cross-tabs can be very powerful in helping an audience see underlying patterns; think about which ones have the best chance of amplifying a presenter's point.

5. Questions about preferred actions can help meeting sponsors understand what kind of actions they might need to support after the presentation.

6. If the moderator of a panel is willing to develop a few polling questions aligned with each panelist, interactivity can be an effective way of keeping an audience connected to all of the panelists.

4.1

After doing an interactive presentation at a hotel convention center, we discovered that in a nearby room, a health food network marketing company was preparing the room so that 60 potential salespeople could hear a motivational talk by the actor Danny Glover. The representatives of the company did not know what Mr. Glover was going to say, except that he was going to testify about the merits of the product. We demonstrated the technology, and company representatives were intrigued by the way interactivity might warm up the audience for Mr. Glover's remarks. We constructed a short series of experience-based questions that concerned people's health ailments, health food usage patterns, and familiarity with network marketing arrangements. (In a network marketing arrangement, a salesperson promotes the product to their friends and family by talking about their use of it regularly, and also recruits other enthusiastic users to be a part of his or her sales team). The plan was to introduce Mr. Glover, and conduct a five-minute polling exercise just before he gave his testimonial.

One of the questions was about how long each person in the room had been taking health food supplements. In our five minutes of preparation with Mr. Glover, we told him that no matter what the distribution of answers was, he would be able to easily riff on the results. If it turned out that the responses were skewed toward heavy usage, he could praise the crowd for being healthy, and for wanting to spread their helpful attitudes toward health to others. If only a minority of the prospective salespeople were users of supplements themselves, Mr. Glover could humorously comment on their "Do as I say not as I do" perspective. He could talk about the need for the crowd to become customers themselves, and discuss how they would become more effective salespeople if they started using the products they planned to sell.

GUIDELINES TO KEEP IN MIND:

- In most instances, someone other than the presenter should be the polling facilitator.
- Demographic and experience questions have the least risk of striking the wrong note.
- Opinion questions can be useful, but there is the risk of forcing presenters to clarify their opinions on issues they might prefer to avoid.
- Fact questions should be approached with caution since the meeting organizer or the person creating the polling questions may not use the same reference sources as the presenter; differences in what are considered facts may be distracting to the participants.
- Consider the risks of asking and displaying post-presentation evaluation questions, including embarrassing the presenter or the meeting sponsor if the audience has a mixed rating of the presentation.

SPEAKER SCENARIO 2:
MODERATE CONTACT WITH SPEAKER
Allowing Moderate Integration of Content and Polling

4.2

The U.S. Coast Guard engaged us to augment a keynote presentation at a conference on sexual assault in the military. The Coast Guard wanted some before and after questions that might show learning gain. The keynote speaker was a very busy consultant and it was rather difficult to find a mutually convenient time for a telephone call. After several email exchanges and one phone conversation, we developed a few polling questions on key facts in the presentation. While the presenter was not allowed to officially advocate for policies about how to adjudicate assault claims, she was also interested in knowing whether opinions on this issue shifted as a result of her talk. After reviewing her presentation slides and having a few conversations, we developed a set of new polling questions that allowed the speaker and the client to see both learning gain and the degree of shift in opinion about how assault claims should be handled. It turned out that the participants had a substantial gain in knowledge but experienced little changes in their preferred policy approach.

GUIDELINES TO KEEP IN MIND:

- Does the presenter think that there are any demographic factors that tend to affect people's perspective on the most relevant issues?
- Are there experiences that the participants might have that the presenter thinks are relevant to what he or she plans to say?
- What are important facts about the presenter's topic that most people do not know? Would it be helpful to ask questions about these facts before the talk? If so, would it be better to reveal the correct answer during polling or not?
- Are there issues where it would be helpful to assess the group's opinion before the presentation begins?
- Is post-presentation polling desirable? If so, should there be any questions that are asked before and after the presentation?

4.2

We were engaged to augment a meeting focused on fostering networking between minority students and alumni at a prestigious graduate business school. The meeting featured a presentation by a business school professor whose topic was the importance of mentoring programs in overall career success and happiness. The professor had never used SPEIK before, and was excited by the opportunity to integrate the technology into his talk.

Through several conversations with us, the professor and our team decided to use the audience polling at three different places in his presentation. At the beginning of the meeting, our team facilitated some polling questions that focused on participants' demographics and their experiences with mentoring programs. About one-third of the way through his presentation, the professor polled attendees about the value they had received from mentoring programs. These questions provided a segue into a short presentation about research findings about the different benefits that mentors and protégés receive from mentoring. Two-thirds of the way through the presentation, he polled participants on the critical success factors in mentoring programs. The questions served as a transition to his discussion of the social science research on this issue.

GUIDELINES TO KEEP IN MIND:

- Which questions are best asked before the presentation starts because they set a good context for the entire speech or because the issues in the questions will be referred to in the first third of the presentation?
- Are there key points in the presentation—these could be anecdotes, facts, or concepts—that would be strengthened by having SPEIK questions just before or after them?
- How many times is the speaker or moderator willing to manage transitions from delivering content to asking SPEIK questions?
- Given the topic, the audience, and the setting, are there points where the audience may experience speaker fatigue, and would welcome a respite from the delivery of information or energy of group interaction? Alternatively, is there a point at which the audience may grow tired of interactivity, and would probably just want the speaker to get on with the content?

USING SPEIK TO IMPROVE CONFERENCES

Strategically-designed audience interactivity can add a great deal to the experience of the participants at a conference, and can significantly boost what conference planners and sponsors gain from the gathering. As you will see, the strongest argument for the use of SPEIK is that it be employed at the beginning of a conference, because a well-designed polling experience can increase participants' sense of connection to the group. This chapter will also discuss the ways in which SPEIK can help conclude a conference, and how it can be used to assist with important adjustments while the conference is going on.

4.3

At the beginning of a conference for conflict resolution professionals, we conducted a plenary session to reinforce a sense of community and to raise some important themes that might not otherwise emerge at the conference. After a number of "Who is Here?" questions (for example, age, region, ethnicity, tenure in the line of work, income, among others) the attendees were asked to provide their assessment of the overall quality of national dialogue about difficult community issues. After seeing the collective results, the participants were invited to have a 10-minute discussion at their tables about the reasons they voted as they did.

After the discussion, the same question was polled again, and the pre- and post-discussion votes were compared. To the surprise of most in the group, people's assessment of the quality of dialogue in the nation was more negative after having talked with each other. In other words, after they discussed the question with their colleagues, they became more cynical. Dialogue made the professionals who promote dialogue become more pessimistic about the national state of dialogue! The irony of this was both amusing and dismaying to the group. The finding was referred to a number of times during the rest of the conference.

> **CONFERENCE SCENARIO 1:**
> ASKING "WHO IS HERE?"
> AT THE START OF A CONFERENCE

> **HOW SPEIK CAN HELP:**

1. A well-executed "Who is here?" session to start a conference helps people connect with their fellow attendees; fostering networking and connectedness is often the primary purpose of such an event.

2. A participatory session at the beginning of a conference sends an important, positive message to attendees about opportunities for participation.

3. An audience polling session can help raise important issues that may be roiling beneath the surface among conference participants.

4. Conference sponsors can get direct information about the degree to which their outreach strategy has reached intended target audiences.

5. The conference-planning team can potentially get information that may allow them to make adjustments to the conference that will help the attendees have a better experience.

On many occasions—often when our session had been added at the last minute—people have told us that the opening conference session was the highlight of their conference.

In designing a SPEIK session for the start of a conference, it is useful to start with the recognition that the session can pursue four somewhat distinct goals. It will be important to decide which goals are most important, and which should be pursued within the timeframe of the session.

GUIDELINES TO KEEP IN MIND:

- If the conference is not based on an existing community (such as a conference for a newly-forming national association) it can be helpful to ask questions that build connections and that illustrate how people share similarities within the context of the conference and perhaps outside of it.
- If the conference builds upon a community that already exists (for example, an annual meeting of a division of a corporation) there is more room to ask questions that build upon community knowledge and shared experiences. There also may be more room for the questions to be humorous, provocative, or otherwise attention-getting.
- To illustrate, one sometimes fun and useful question in a "Who is here?" session is to inquire about people's motivation for coming to the conference.

Your approach to designing questions that pursue the goal of increasing the group's self-knowledge is somewhat different depending on the context of the group. The following example illustrates the kind of question that might be used in service of this goal in a newly forming community.

Example 1.1

SCENARIO:

A peace activist conference for a new organization

QUESTION:

Which of these were your strongest motivations for coming to the conference?

1. Be energized by meeting peace activists from other parts of the world.
2. Take a break from the conflicts in my area.
3. It was a time for a long trip.
4. Learn other peace building techniques.
5. Needed to use some frequent flyer miles.
6. Some other reason.

If the group is already established, you can design questions that assume more commonality, or that are more playful or "edgy".

Example 1.2

SCENARIO:

An annual sales division meeting

QUESTION:

Which of these were your strongest motivations for coming to the conference?

1. To learn better techniques for doing my job.
2. My boss is here—absence was an option, but not a smart one.
3. To learn more about the other side of the sales/marketing force.
4. Despite what they say...I think Chicago is really nice in November!
5. I am here for the same reason everyone else is here (whatever that is).
6. There are some folks I really like reconnecting with every year, if you know what I mean.

GOAL 2:
BUILD ANTICIPATION ABOUT THE CONFERENCE EXPERIENCE.

GUIDELINES TO KEEP IN MIND:

- The entire sequence of polling questions provides a platform from which to review the agenda of the conference, and do so in a way that engages the participants.
- Conference organizers can use polling questions to direct participant attention to specific elements of the conference that they think are under-appreciated.
- Polling questions can be used to remind participants of the variety of opportunities that the conference presents that are not on the agenda, such as networking and caucus group formation.

Example 2.1

SCENARIO:
Focus on formal conference sessions

QUESTION:
Which of these conference elements are you most looking forward to?

1. Skill-building sessions.
2. Workshops.
3. Plenary sessions.
4. Exhibition.
5. Ask the expert sessions.

Example 2.2

SCENARIO:

Focus on structured conference community building elements

QUESTION:

Which of these aspects of the conference are you most looking forward to?

1. Substantive conference sessions.
2. The chance to network at the formal receptions.
3. Evening forays into the community.
4. Informal networking during meals.

GOAL 3:
DRAW OUT DIVERSITY OF EXPERIENCE/OPINION ON A SUBSTANTIVE ISSUE.

GUIDELINES TO KEEP IN MIND:

- Polling questions can provide a way to raise important issues that the conference planners or sponsors think conference participants need to discuss, whether or not these issues are directly reflected in the conference agenda.
- If you are not deeply connected to the group, it is possible to inadvertently raise hot button issues during an early polling session focused on conference content. It is usually best to have a small group of people review the polling questions to ensure this will not happen.
- Consider asking a substantive polling question to the entire group, having them engage in short conversation with a few people, then polling the group again to examine potential changes of opinion. This can be extremely effective in establishing an issue as the central discussion theme of a conference.
- Asking questions about personal issues can work very well to deepen connectedness if it strikes the right tone. The type of question in Example 3.1 could be perceived as productively deepening people's connectedness, or as being inappropriate for the setting. For example, that question might work very well for the peace activist conference referenced earlier (1.1) but might not work for the sales force gathering (1.2). When considering this option, think carefully about the culture of the group, the person facilitating the session, and the depth and tone of such questions.

Example 3.1

SCENARIO:

Focus on deepening connections between conference attendees

QUESTION:

Which of these challenges has your family confronted in the last year?

1. Physical or mental health difficulties.
2. School or employment difficulties.
3. Loved ones passing away.
4. Major relationship setbacks.
5. Something else very important.

GOAL 4:
GENERATE INFORMATION FOR CONFERENCE SPONSORS.

GUIDELINES TO KEEP IN MIND:

- Talk to conference sponsors/planners to determine what questions they want to know about for future planning.
- Have them prioritize their list. Remind them that the final list should balance their interest in questions that help the sponsor with future planning and ones that enhance the participant experience in the room.
- In most cases, it is empowering to provide the participants with the reasons why their answers are important to the conference planners. At the same time, it is important not to over-promise about the level of influence the participants are likely to have.

Kerry Wade
Neighborhood District Coordinator
City of Seattle, Washington

Ms. Wade has been using SPEIK for several years in her work doing community outreach for local government agencies.

When did you start using audience response devices?

I started using them when I worked for neighborhood planning. We wanted to get more active engagement from the historically under-represented communities. Our planning processes had been dominated by what might be called mainstream voices who have always had access to power. We wanted to gather the information in a way that was scientific and where we could provide some type of interpretation for people who did not speak English at all, and who may not even be able to read in their own language.

So we put the questions up in English, and used translation equipment to make sure everyone could participate in their own language. We used the clickers in this way to do community health assessments both at places like the Somali Community Center where we only translated into one language and at general meetings for everybody where we had translation into thirteen languages. We have done this for other topics besides community health, such as for the police chief search, for the Department of Transportation, and other departments.

It seems like many folks around Seattle use the devices. How did this happen?

We first started using a very old set that the auditor's department had. Once I knew how well they worked and wanted to get some new ones, I decided to try to spread the cost around. The remotes we have cost about $50 each and the receiver cost $700, so we had to raise about $7,000 to get 100 devices and two receivers. After people heard how well they worked, I went to different departments to fundraise. I said, "It's the end of the budget year, you need to spend some money down. You know that you will want to use them. Just spare a little money and you will get priority for borrowing them." The groups that bought in were the City Council, the Department of Planning and Development, the Office of Civil Rights, the Department of Transportation, the Seattle Public Utilities, the Department of Neighborhoods, the Office of Sustainability, and maybe one more department. And the Department of Public Health didn't contribute money, but they use them a lot. I have trained people all over the city in how to use them.

What do you think is the next step for your use of technology?

I am an outreach person and engagement person. So my thing is "What are the barriers to participation and engagement?" The fact is: not everybody can come to a meeting, and most people who can't come to a meeting are moms, people who work long hours, and so on. My job is engagement, not just getting information; so what is the best way to create engagement? I know there are a lot of people who care about these issues who cannot come. We do these on-line town halls where we let them answer the questions remotely so that they can answer the questions, and participate in the meeting, even if they can't be there. That is why I love some of the app-based systems for people's phones. So you have what is happening in the room, and you can make the room bigger for folks who can't be there.

Any key lessons that you want to share?

It is important to think through both the wording of questions and whether you choose to show answers. And people will surprise you. At one meeting, we asked a wonky question that was something like: "What type of transportation do you use to get food that you prepare at home?" To save time, this was going to be one of the questions we did not show the answers to. But people insisted on seeing the answer. It turned out that 70 percent of the people used their cars. Basically they have a food desert, and I was not acknowledging that. We also asked how long it took them to get to the store. They wanted to see the answer because they were thinking: we are going to be able to use this to advocate for our neighborhood.

CONFERENCE SCENARIO 2:
ASKING "HOW ARE WE DOING?" QUESTIONS
AT PLENARY SESSIONS
DURING A CONFERENCE

HOW SPEIK CAN HELP:

1. If the gathering already has a mid-conference plenary on the agenda, an interactive "How are we doing?" session can give conference planners valuable information, and help participants feel like their voices count. For example, conference attendees might be probed on their agreement with the statement: As a whole, we are avoiding or downplaying the key issues that will affect our success as a group over the next year.

2. Using SPEIK as a check-in mid-conference can offer a good way of helping conference managers make small adjustments, such as temperature of conference rooms, timing of workshops, and the pace or amount of interaction time during sessions.

GUIDELINES TO KEEP IN MIND:

- Do not ask process questions on issues about which no adjustments can be made.
- If a few passionate people claim an issue is emerging at a conference, polling mid-conference allows this claim to be objectively and transparently investigated.
- If polling questions are going to be used to probe emergent controversial issues, be careful to frame the question so that people on different sides of controversies will experience the question as fair.

HOW SPEIK CAN HELP:

1. People may be more likely to answer evaluation questions if doing so is built into the structure of the conference.

2. The answers to the evaluation questions are already in a computer database, and do not have to be entered manually.

3. If the evaluation session asks a few key demographic/ experience questions (or if people have the same device they used at the beginning of the conference), it will be possible to run cross-tabs in the post-meeting analysis to determine if some conference participants had a different experience of the conference than others.

GUIDELINES TO KEEP IN MIND:

- The display of the results makes the evaluation of the conference more transparent.
- Consider the feelings of people in the room and those who have left (for example, presenters) when considering whether to display results or not. While we generally think that more information is better, there are times when displaying results could make some people in the room feel publicly shamed.
- If results are not displayed, people will be curious about them. Expect that people will more than likely have follow-up inquiries about the results than if you do the evaluation in the traditional written way. Think through a useful response that will address these inquiries.

Kerry Wade
Neighborhood District Coordinator
City of Seattle, Washington

Ms. Wade has used SPEIK technology hundreds of times. These are a few of her best practice tips.

Best Practices for Using SPEIK for Feedback

- You can ask too many questions.
- You do not need to show every result.
- Know ahead of time which results will be interesting, and show those. (People almost always want to know age, for example.)
- For a public meeting, you may not want to have people sign out the clickers, since they might have the legitimate concern that someone can probe the open meeting records and find out how they voted on things.
- It is very helpful to get clickers that allow the branding of slides, so that sponsors get credit during the process.
- Even if the clicker system has limited translation to other languages, consider using drop in images of translated text for options to questions. You can potentially translate questions to languages that the program does not directly support.

USING SPEIK TO IMPROVE WORKSHOPS

We are defining a workshop as a session where the focus of the meeting organizer is to create an exchange—perhaps brief, perhaps extended—among the people in the room. This is in contrast to a speech or panel, which is focused on one-way communication between presenters and the audience. A conference is an entirely different matter, since the defining characteristic of a conference involves multiple independent sessions that might be organized as speeches, workshops, or perhaps other formats.

Workshops can be organized any number of ways. For the sake of this discussion, we will focus on settings that are devoted to the Crosstalk mode, since the other modes have already been covered.

Kevin Bomhoff
Facilitator and Strategic Development Director
Wichita State University Center for Community Support and Research

Mr. Bomhoff witnessed a SPEIK demonstration at a large meeting of non-profit managers.

What do you want to say about the demonstration of the polling technology a few days ago?

Well, I saw the engagement. I thought it was funny because some people wanted their votes to be counted so much that they were holding their little clicker up and we were told that we didn't need to do that but—what I saw in that was people expressing that "My vote needs to count!" In our large group facilitation work we end up doing a lot of dots voting processes which oftentimes we don't engage everyone in the process. And we're not getting that feedback immediately. We're saying "we'll get back to you about the results" or "this is generally what it looks like." I don't know how much of a trustworthy process that creates. And what I saw happening in that room was you could trust that; that's what was really happening in real time.

A few years ago, we were asked to facilitate a meeting in the aftermath of the weekend killing of a high school football player through gang violence; the young man had had no previous gang involvement. That Monday, the level of grief, shock, and anger among the student population was so intense that the school was put on lockdown and a heavy police presence was called out. Through the course of the next few days, many adults descended upon the school to support the students. At some point, administrators realized that nothing had been done to directly support the teammates of the murdered youth. We were called in to design and lead a teammates-only session in which participants could talk about their feelings. We decided that anonymous polling might be a useful on-ramp to the discussion.

The warm-up question was focused on a recent game against their major rival school. They had beaten the team pretty badly, which was a surprise to everyone, given each team's previous record. Our question was: "What did you really think was going to happen in the game?" The answers essentially ranged from "I was very sure we would get crushed" to "I was very sure that we would crush them." The question did at least two important things: First, it brought a collective success to mind, which was a mood lifter. Second, the ability to anonymously answer the question gave players room to reveal pre-game feelings of doubt that there had been pressure against admitting.

After the laughter died down at seeing how many of them had carried some secret doubts, the polling questions turned to the topic of the meeting, which probed topics such as their previous experience with death, their exposure to community violence, how well they knew the deceased, and their current emotional state. These questions gave these seemingly tough football players a safe venue for admitting whatever feelings they had that they might be reluctant to admit, including anger, fear, indifference, or being overwhelmed. A football assistant coach who had publicly criticized SPEIK at community meetings as a "game show gimmick" subsequently said that the anonymous polling was a brilliant way of starting the conversation.

Whether SPEIK is being used or not, it is useful for facilitators to be clear at any point about the intention of the group they are trying to support. If polling devices are used, this clarity about purpose is particularly important, so that the facilitators ask the right questions at the right time to support the group at that moment.

HOW SPEIK CAN HELP:

1. Regardless of workshop type, SPEIK makes it possible to increase the number of people actively contributing to the meeting. The decision about how many people can have a say in the process can be less driven by ideas about efficient communication and more by a strategic analysis about which perspectives need to be present. Most people would agree that if more than 10 people are at a meeting, it becomes very difficult to hear the thoughts from each person. With SPEIK, it does not matter how large the meeting is—everyone can be heard as long as you ask the right questions.

2. SPEIK increases the accuracy and detail of responses of a group; this can be helpful even in relatively small groups.

3. Cross-tabs are particularly relevant when you are trying to get people to talk to each other. For example, we once used a SPEIK session to help a set of managers in diverse parts of a large corporation better understand an attrition problem. Polling data showed that younger people had a somewhat different perception of the problem than older meeting attendees. The fact that age clearly impacted perceptions of the issue appeared to make it easier for people with a different sense of issues to talk productively with each other.

4. If there are more topics that are important to discuss than time to do so, polling can allow the group to make its own decision about what topics to spend time on. In a meeting aimed largely at giving the group responsibility for its communication and relationships, using SPEIK questions to have participants control their experience may be particularly empowering.

Delia Carmen
Associate Director for Equity and Inclusion
Annie. E. Casey Foundation

Ms Carmen witnessed a demonstration of SPEIK at a conference focused on equity, inclusion, and diversity work.

In doing work on equity, diversity and inclusion, it's a very difficult conversation. You have people sitting in the room who don't see this as their issue, or don't agree, or who are silent. I think this is a great way of engaging people and taking the temperature of the room. Opposing views could be heard without feeling that people are called out directly; the technology almost forces them to stay with the conversation, since they want to be heard. Then you can have a real dialogue.

USING SPEIK FOR SORTING THROUGH OPTIONS FOR ACTION

In most groups, important decisions about direction are not made through a democratic process but by a leader or set of leaders who feel that they have more time or capacity to analyze a series of options and assess trade-offs. Nevertheless, it can often be useful to have a larger number of people provide feedback.

The simplest way of getting a group to give feedback on a set of potential actions is to ask which action they would most recommend. ("Which of the following five options for action would you most recommend?") When a question is asked this way, what results is a collective assessment of possible actions. However, what cannot be determined is whether people have used similar criteria to make those choices.

In contrast to asking one summary recommendation question, we have found a better way to find out what a group thinks about a set of possible actions. We have developed what we call the *3-E Question Scrub*; it is based on asking the group to assess a set of actions against three criteria:

3-E QUESTION SCRUB CRITERIA:

EFFECTIVENESS > Which of these actions, if executed well, would be most effective in addressing our problem?

EASE > Which of these actions would be the easiest to execute well?

ENERGY/ ENTHUSIASM > Which of these actions would naturally generate the most energy/ enthusiasm from the people needed to make it happen?

The *3-E Question Scrub* works because each of these criteria is important but they inherently have very little to do with each other. (One could imagine using a different set of criteria that reflect other priorities.) We have seen cases in which the group's top choices for each of the scrub questions are different. However, when an action emerges as a top item on two or three of the scrub questions, most groups find this gives them powerful guidance about what should be done, and why.

When SPEIK is used in this way, it is usually a good idea to convey to the group the degree of influence that the group is likely to have over the actual decision. Typically, when a meeting sponsor harnesses the collective brainpower of a meeting using audience polling, the sponsor does not engage in absolute democracy; rather, the group is serving in an advisory capacity about what the group's priorities should be. (In the language of Chapter 2, the group is serving as counselors not collaborators.) To avoid creating expectations that will not be met, it is usually best to remind people that this exercise is not equivalent to making the decision. In such settings, it is often important to refer to the interactive process as "polling," instead of "voting," as an additional reminder.

A NOTE ABOUT GROUP SIZE

We recognize that often it is not possible to predict the size of the audience. SPEIK can be used with a range of participants.

- The value of polling starts at about eight or nine people; at that size, conducting a poll begins to take less time than tallying a group's responses using other, more traditional methods.
- In a small group, the ability to improvise questions is likely to be important as new issues emerge in the conversation. Prepare yourself and the group for this possibility.
- The smaller the group, the more likely it is that someone will question the use of SPEIK; be prepared to articulate the reasons for deploying it. One of the explanations that most people find compelling is the way in which SPEIK protects people's anonymity and thus increases the candor of people's expressed opinions.
- When the size of the group gets to about 15 people, there is no other strategy for reading the room that is as efficient and accurate as SPEIK.

5.
USING SPEIK IN UNEXPECTED CIRCUMSTANCES

5

Unexpected

Circumstances change and the extent to which SPEIK is useful should be noted. How might SPEIK technology be used in settings that might be considered unexpected or unusual? As we have gone about the United States and around the world evangelizing about the power of SPEIK technology, one notion that many people have is that SPEIK devices are only appropriate in the context of institutional or community-based meetings that are relatively large, as in 30 or more people.

Our experience has led us to different conclusions, namely:

- SPEIK technology can indeed be very useful in small group situations;
- SPEIK can be used to productively augment events that are primarily social in nature.

In this chapter, we will briefly review some of the most important lessons for using the technology for "work" events when the group size is relatively small, and for settings that are primarily social events.

WORK SETTINGS

Our use of SPEIK in small group settings with a work purpose is best characterized as comprising the three modes of the workshops described in Chapter 2. In some cases, we have used SPEIK in the context of focus group meetings, where the purpose of the encounter was to solicit and assess reactions from the participants. This fits the Feedback modality discussed previously. In other circumstances, we used SPEIK to bolster the conversation among participants. This use is closest to the Crosstalk mode described in Chapter 2. Because the use of the devices in these settings is different, we will present our lessons for each of these settings separately.

Focus Groups

Most experts in focus groups suggest that the maximum size of a focus group should be about 10 to 12 people. If the questions for groups of this size only have two or three answers—for example, "are you in favor, do you like, dislike, or are neutral about this advertisement?"—a show of hands is faster then SPEIK. But if it is useful to have a more fine-grained response to the stimuli (for example, from strongly like to strongly dislike), and it is useful to have a conversation, SPEIK's efficiency in making quick assessments can have advantages. Importantly, with SPEIK, it is possible to increase the size of the group and still retain the ability to have focused follow-up conversations.

HOW SPEIK CAN HELP:

1. You can more quickly and precisely know the diversity of perspectives in the room, which can help you make better choices in how much time to spend following up on different points.

2. Focus groups can be about twice as large without losing the capacity for targeted exploration of comments.

3. The display of answers helps reinforce the idea that all perspectives are useful.

4. You can get quick feedback data on a large number of stimuli if that is your goal.

5. Cross-tabulations (real time or post-meeting) can help illuminate some drivers of opinion.

GUIDELINES TO KEEP IN MIND:

- It may be valuable to have a specific order of topics and associated questions that you will take the group through.
- While it is helpful to have two people facilitating, it is not difficult for one person to successfully manage the session.
- It may be useful to remind the group that even though the SPEIK devices may be set up anonymously, your expectation is that people will be willing to explain why they answered the polling questions the way they did.

5.1

One client was interested in getting feedback about what kind of language about policies might be most helpful in persuading progressives and conservatives to favor policies that pursued social equity. The client gathered a group of professionals to express how attractive or unattractive they found different statements. Within two hours, we were able to get reactions to dozens of statements. In addition, we were able to use the post-event cross-tabulation feature to determine which statements generated disparate responses depending on age, ideology, or other factors.

Small Group Dialogue Sessions

The discussion in Chapter 2 based on workshops in Crosstalk mode was grounded on the presumption that the groups would be large enough where SPEIK would have clear advantages in efficiency in conducting quick polls that could be used to guide facilitation choices. When the group is small enough—say between 8 to 15 people—other methods of surveying such as showing hands are similar in speed, there can still be advantages in using SPEIK that should be considered.

HOW SPEIK CAN HELP:

1. Sometimes, groups have an internal culture that defines some perspectives as less acceptable than others. By using SPEIK, you can broaden the range of responses that are considered legitimate.

2. The technology allows a way for people to express their perspective without being unduly influenced by what other people have expressed.

3. People can submit their responses anonymously and discover that they are not the only person who feels that way. This can be particularly important in settings in which there are power differentials in a small group (such as an executive board).

GUIDELINES TO KEEP IN MIND:

- In a small group, protecting anonymity is possible, but may require specific strategies. For example, one option is to not display the number of people who have voted in real-time.
- It is often best not to advance the group through a pre-determined sequence of questions, but instead think of the questions as a menu of choices that you will select from as the need arises.
- There may be a need to develop new questions on the fly in response to the conversation that emerges.
- It is often useful to have a co-facilitator, so that one person can attend to the creation or choice of keypad questions while the other keeps attention on the group.

5.2

We were asked to help a liberal seminary that had recently had turmoil over issues of diversity and inclusion. The issue was so highly charged that some people told us privately that they knew others had given false responses to questions on anonymous surveys that asked for their ethnic group in order to push collective results in one direction or another. We had been told numerous times that many people did not feel safe to publicly articulate their opinion about the level of progress the campus had made on these issues.

We arranged to have a small group dialogue (about 10 people) of an ethnically diverse gathering. Our approach was to construct a series of questions on which there might be disagreement (such as, "How would you assess the level of commitment by the campus administration to inclusion of evangelical students?") and to display the range of answers. If there was substantial agreement, we might only talk about the question briefly. If there was significant divergence of views, we covered the lens on the projector so that the results did not become a distraction. Then we facilitated a discussion focused on the implications of the diversity of viewpoints in the group. People were able to talk about why they might have different views without declaring their personal opinions. We were subsequently told that this strategy created a much higher degree of safety than other dialogues that had been attempted on these topics.

CELEBRATIONS, REUNIONS, AND OTHER SOCIAL EVENTS

So far, our discussion of SPEIK has framed polling as a powerful, perhaps even transformative, supplement to the main activity of a speech or panel, workshop, dialogue, focus group, or conference. Typically, these settings are created in the context of an institution pursuing some long-run objective beyond the encounter. But SPEIK can also be used at social events as a method of making the event more engaging. On many occasions, we have created what might be called a "polling show" that provided a new way for a group to experience the enjoyment of being together. We have done this at birthday parties, family and school reunions, contests for art or fashion, and even at mixers for singles. In fact, Matthew facilitated a polling show during a part of David's wedding reception.

We will briefly describe some of the things we have learned about using SPEIK in social settings. Before we do this, let's do a quick review of the four primary types of SPEIK questions; this time, we will highlight the impact of the questions when the overall context of the gathering is essentially celebrating someone or something (for instance, a person, an organization, place, or event) and/or building a sense of community.

Demographic Questions

People enjoy seeing evidence that there are a variety of people in a group. We have found that demonstrations of diversity at a celebration tend to reflect positively on whatever entity is the focus of the celebration. Even if the group is largely homogenous on the classic diversity dimensions—age, race, gender, sexual orientation, and so on—it is often possible to find some less obvious dimensions that will cause people to have a moment of appreciation for the diversity that is in the room. Some examples of demographic characteristics that can be useful in this way are neighborhood, religion, country of ancestry, or occupation.

Fact Questions

In the context of a celebratory event, questions that highlight factual knowledge serve two primary purposes. First, they can become a point of focus for teaching or reminding the group of some key facts about the entity being celebrated. Second, because SPEIK can be programmed for competitions, fact questions are the primary means by which individuals or groups can have a fun competitive game about how much they know about that entity. Some SPEIK systems even have Jeopardy!-style templates that are built into the software to assist in the development of competitions.

Experience Questions

SPEIK makes it possible to query participants about whether they have had specific types of experiences directly with the celebrated honoree (person, organization, place, event, and so on). Experience questions can be constructed to highlight the diverse ways in which the crowd has become familiar with the honoree. Such a set of questions also has the impact of informing or reminding everyone about different characteristics of the honoree.

Opinion Questions

In creating an opinion question—especially when celebrating people—one can strike a wide variety of tones, from elevating ("If Denise were a luxury car, what kind would she be?"), to empathetic ("Which of these triumphs in Tim's life most touched you when you heard about it?"), to gently chiding ("Which of these characteristics of Wayne is the biggest impediment to marriage possibilities?"). There is a lot of room for creativity with these questions. Some lessons we have learned follow.

5.3

A few years ago, we created a polling show for a 50th birthday party that included about 75 people. The guests included people with a very broad range of familiarity with the honoree. The polling slides included all four major question types. The honoree had taken a sabbatical earlier in his life to join a few hundred miles, weeks-long march. One question we included was "Which of these exciting journeys did Steve take during his sabbatical?" For people who did not know the honoree well, the question prompted them to make an inference about what kind of journey Steve might take. For party guests who had known Steve very well, the question prompted a fond memory of talking to Steve about his adventure.

After people answered the question but before the correct answer was revealed, the facilitator asked a few people who voted for incorrect answers to explain their thinking. Then anyone who voted correctly was asked what they remembered about the conversation with Steve about the trip. The question created an extended moment when a few people had the chance to make a brief positive and/or humorous comment about the honoree, and in the end, everyone learned an actual fact about him.

SOCIAL EVENTS SCENARIO 1:
PARTIES CELEBRATING PEOPLE, ORGANIZATIONS, EVENTS, OR PLACES

HOW SPEIK CAN HELP:

1. Polling creates a moment where everyone is doing something together and not just observing.

2. SPEIK can help the group take delight in its diversity of connections to the honoree.

3. The celebration is less dependent on toasts and roasts, which can be of variable quality.

4. Everyone is given a chance to express him or herself.

5. Audience polling helps guests learn more about the honoree.

6. SPEIK can strengthen people's emotional connection with the honoree.

GUIDELINES TO KEEP IN MIND:

In designing a polling question, ask whether the polling question will make the audience:

- Laugh.
- Elevate the honoree.
- Empathize with the honoree.
- Reflect on and/or make a brief comment about the honoree, or about the audience itself.

Of course, many questions may accomplish more than one of these goals. Remember, questions that might work very well at the birthday party for a forest ranger might be very unsuccessful at a party for a Wall Street attorney. As you design a mix of questions, do so in light of the occasion, the way the honoree likes to be appreciated, and the relationship of the guests to the honoree.

We have found that the SPEIK show celebrating a person is best concluded with a final question that has been intentionally designed to get a strong super-majority of people to unite on one answer that elevates the honoree. An example might be:

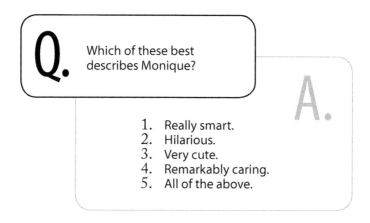

Q. Which of these best describes Monique?

A.

1. Really smart.
2. Hilarious.
3. Very cute.
4. Remarkably caring.
5. All of the above.

While a few people might answer one, two, three, or four, most people will know that the answer they are supposed to choose is number five. The impact of seeing an overwhelming number of people answer a question in this way feels like the electronic equivalent of everyone clapping for the person.

Because you have commanded the audience's collective attention, you should guide them to the next activity after the last polling question. Do not let the moment fall flat without a plan for what comes next.

SOCIAL EVENTS SCENARIO 2:
CLASS REUNIONS

HOW SPEIK CAN HELP:

1. Audience polling provides a way for all gathered to have a collective moment of togetherness that involves participation, not just listening.

2. SPEIK can provide a fun way for everyone to remember their experience of something (for example, sporting contests, faculty gaffes, student pranks, dramatic events, trends, and customs) that is widely known. People will both revel in the memories but also may enjoy discovering that different people remember the events very differently.

3. Team competitions based on old distinctions—like where people used to live—or new ones—such as parental status—can heighten the energy in the room.

GUIDELINES TO KEEP IN MIND:

- Make sure that the questions are based on broadly shared knowledge, not just what a small group of friends might know.
- To create good questions, it may be necessary to gather a small committee of people from different sub-groups to ensure that questions will have broad resonance.
- The SPEIK show can include some fact questions that are scored for competition as well as experience or opinion questions that are simply there for fun.
- Think through whether some questions have the chance of opening old psychological wounds.

SOCIAL EVENTS SCENARIO 3:
FAMILY REUNIONS

HOW SPEIK CAN HELP:

1. Provides a moment of active togetherness for the entire group.

2. Helps remind or teach people about family events or relatives they may have forgotten.

3. Uses group competitions to create interactions between people whose connection may be weak or non-existent.

4. Prompts poignant memories or elicits comments.

GUIDELINES TO KEEP IN MIND:

- Again, be mindful about opening old wounds.
- Basing questions on old pictures can be a very effective way of sparking memories or creating moments of laughter.
- If you want to use questions to prompt comments, it is a good idea to have a couple of confederates in the reunion who you have prepared to make brief, heartfelt comments. If you arrange that they do this early in the show, it will probably be useful to point out to the group how their heartfelt but brief comment allowed the entire process to keep moving. ("That comment was really great! Not only did you really capture something great and true about Grandma, but it was really short…so we can keep this moving.")
- Pay attention to people's reactions to question prompts; sometimes an effective follow-up query that is not a polling question can create a powerful moment for the family. ("Carl, you seemed to have a reaction to that picture of Aunt Jean; what do you remember most about her?").

There have been many times when we have used SPEIK to serve as an icebreaker at a social event. For example, on several occasions, we have provided a "Sex Trivia" game at a singles mixer. The use here is similar to deploying the devices at an opening of a conference; the design goal is to create a polling experience that is both fun and memorable, and that might serve as a useful conversation starter for the rest of the gathering.

HOW SPEIK CAN HELP:

1. Provides a non-threatening platform for people to speak to strangers.

2. Lightens the atmosphere by creating fun.

3. If you allow for it, the responses to the SPEIK questions can foster cross-talk or comments to the full group.

"...the design goal for an icebreaker is to create a fun experience that is a useful conversation starter."

- Since you will need to persuade people to take part in an activity that is unusual and may need explanation, recruit a small team of people willing to coax others into participating. Such a team can prepare the audience by distributing devices or preparing them to use their own devices.
- There is a fine line between questions that are edgy and those that make people uncomfortable.
- Random teams (such as season of birth) can work well enough to create a mild spirit of competition that enhances the event. Consider whether there might be value in basing the competition on affinity groups that are rather natural, like age and gender. (At one professional singles mixer, the teams were older women, older men, younger men, and younger women). It is also acceptable to bring some creativity to team assignments to produce affinity groups that are unexpected, like ones based on length of time living in the area.

SOCIAL EVENTS SCENARIO 5:
CONTESTS

Because of its ability to tally preferences quickly, SPEIK is a highly effective method of facilitating a contest where people are judging the prize worthiness of entries. We have used the technology for visual art contests where the entire audience was transformed into a judging panel, as well as in settings where the technology augmented the deliberations of a small panel of contest judges during fashion shows.

HOW SPEIK CAN HELP:

1. If the answers are not immediately displayed, SPEIK can allow an entire audience to assess the relative merit of submissions without embarrassing the people associated with submissions that do not get strong support.

2. The technology makes it feasible for a very large number of people to participate in prize selection.

3. Having a "people's choice" award can supplement or even replace awards by expert judges, giving event attendees a greater stake in the contest.

4. SPEIK can be used to augment panel deliberations. For instance, at a fashion show, a panel of four judges used the technology to quickly determine their five most favored entries from a very large number, after which they engaged in extensive discussion to determine the top prizes.

GUIDELINES TO KEEP IN MIND:

- Not showing the poll results publicly prevents embarrassment of weak vote-getters.
- Animations can allow the display of multiple visual objects at once, which helps people make better comparisons because they can see them all simultaneously.

PART 3:
REFLECTIONS

6.
CREATING THE PARADIGM SHIFT

6
Shift

In Part 1 of the book, we tried to persuade you that SPEIK represents a new approach to meetings that you should implement and generally support. In Part 2, we reviewed some practical advice about how to use the technology in different types of meetings; this advice evolved through the hundreds of SPEIK experiences we have collectively created. The chance to work on these meetings have also pushed us to create a checklist of tasks that are far too detailed for some readers to think about but that are important for other readers. This advice about these points of detail to consider are presented in Appendix 1.

As we close the main part of the book, we want to step back from the details of how to use SPEIK at meetings to discuss some bigger picture reflections about the technology. To re-iterate, we think that SPEIK represents a potential paradigm shift in the nature of meetings and their facilitation and management, and perhaps has some important implications about even larger issues such as democracy within groups and cooperation. Whenever SPEIK starts to become truly widespread, we expect organizational psychologists to explore these issues in more depth than we do in this volume. People who think both practically and philosophically about the nature of human cooperation will find SPEIK worthy of attention when it becomes widespread. We do think that this is inevitable, but could take anywhere from years to decades. In this chapter we offer a few thoughts concerning the potential spread of SPEIK and the kinds of people and sectors we think are most likely to become early adopters. In the next chapter, we put forward some initial thoughts about the values embodied by SPEIK and some of their implications for people and organizations using the technology.

FALSEHOODS THAT IMPEDE THE SPREAD OF SPEIK

The first issue is the relatively slow speed of the dissemination of the technology. The first SPEIK products appeared in the 1970's. It seems to us that there are four beliefs about the technology that are essentially false and that limit people's willingness to explore it.

FALSEHOOD 1:
POLLING SYSTEMS ARE EXPENSIVE

THE TRUTH:

Polling systems based on user devices (such as cell phones, tablets, or laptops), used in a venue with a reasonably high capacity wireless internet and good cell phone coverage, can be temporarily acquired by a presenter at a very modest cost; one company charges as little as $65 for one-time use of an internet tool that can support two simultaneous sessions with each having up to 250 smart input devices. As for standalone devices, one company that sells them has a non-discounted price of $59 per input device and $600 a receiver; a meeting professional can buy enough equipment to provide an unlimited number of meetings for 50 people for less than $4,000.

FALSEHOOD 2:
POLLING SYSTEMS ARE DIFFICULT TO LEARN

THE TRUTH:

Today's systems use an interface very similar to very widely used programs (such as Microsoft Word or PowerPoint) or rely on web-based interfaces.

FALSEHOOD 3:
POLLING SYSTEMS ARE DIFFICULT TO CARRY OR SHIP

THE TRUTH:

As recently as 15 years ago, this was true. Now, input devices (often known as keypads or clickers) are no bigger than a television remote control, and may be as small as a very thick credit card. As a result, several dozen standalone input devices can be easily transported in checked or carry-on luggage. People can also ship them easily and inexpensively to themselves or to a colleague with whom one might be sharing ownership and use. And with increasing numbers of systems based on users' devices (or BYOD—bring your own device), shipping or carrying devices may become a non-issue in some cases.

FALSEHOOD 4:
POLLING SYSTEMS WILL LEAD TO PRESENTERS LOSING THEIR EMOTION-BASED CONNECTION

THE TRUTH:

It is true that if used poorly, polling systems can focus presenters and audience attention on the technology itself and not on their connection to each other. If used well however, polling systems can boost the cognitive and emotional connection between a presenter and the audience, as well as among the participants of a meeting.

TRENDS IMPACTING SPEIK

As more people get exposed to this technology, we expect that these falsehoods will be believed by fewer and fewer people. In addition, there are some societal trends that all point in the direction of increased use of SPEIK. For example, the increasing ubiquity of reliable internet access has already made SPEIK more widely adopted. Starting around the year 2007, a number of companies (most prominently, PollEverywhere.com) began releasing internet-based SPEIK systems that use the text capacity of cell phones to serve as the input device and the web as the means by which a computer accumulates results and communicates with the projector in the room.

A second technological trend is the integration of personal technology devices into daily life. According to Pew Research, in 2015, 64 percent of all Americans owned a smartphone. We can expect that the technological advances will only increase the trend of people carrying around technology that will allow them to easily communicate with SPEIK systems. There are already companies (for example, PolltoGo.com) that market smartphone apps designed to turn a smartphone into both the input device and the display device of a SPEIK system. And companies that have primarily relied on standalone devices (for example, Turning Technologies) have moved to expand their SPEIK systems to make it easy to integrate user owned devices into a SPEIK experience.

Such trends making SPEIK more available will continue. Even though Google Glass (a set of spectacles projecting an interactive web screen in the vision of the wearer) is largely considered an unsuccessful product, it is highly likely that other somewhat discrete personal display and input technologies will continue to emerge. For example, a number of companies claim to be working on systems that will soon allow your hand to serve as a keypad or keyboard. As more options emerge for accessible display and input options, managing the SPEIK device itself will become less of an issue, which removes another impediment.

A final major trend that we think only augments trends supporting SPEIK usage is the increasing tendency for the collection and analysis of individual feedback. Barely a day goes by where someone does not offer you a chance to add your opinion, whether the source of the request is the receipt at the drug store, the telephone robot that allows you to get to customer service representatives, or television shows like American Idol or Dancing With the Stars. One could argue that it is quite odd how often our opinions are solicited as consumers given how rarely they are quested as group participants.

With people being increasingly familiar with being asked their opinion, each person carrying around an input device, and more recognition that sometimes the best way for a group to tap its wisdom is to get a summary answer that includes many members, we expect that it is only a matter of time until SPEIK use starts gaining more traction in the market for adult meetings.

There is a growing recognition that there may be group collective wisdom in using surveys not just to exploit consumer patterns but also to identify advantages. This appreciation of the value of collective assessment is evident in the trend toward crowdsourcing and other uses of social media to engage many people on problems. There are a number of societal trends that point in the direction of increasing appreciation that there can be a special value in looking at collective or cooperative assessments. Three widely selling books (*The Wisdom of Crowds*, *Smart Mobs*, and *Here Comes Everybody*), each focused on slightly different aspects of the general idea that there is a significant benefit from properly eliciting and leveraging the summaries of group perspectives of a situation.

Our belief is the forces that trend toward more group interactivity, greater engagement, and more usable data will result in increasing use of audience polling. We also believe that as more people have more exposure to audience polling, there will be recognition that audience interactivity adds value to group participants, presenters, and the sponsors who pay for meetings. Our aim is to accelerate this trend towards more interactivity, as well as to raise some important issues that need to be thought about as the use of polling grows.

We would not have written this book if we did not believe that SPEIK should be in use in a wide variety of settings far more than it currently is. While we think that people who care about all types of organizations and meetings would be behooved by considering the role that polling can play in improving encounters, there are some sectors of activity and types of organizations that are particularly well-suited for being an engine for growth of the technology.

SECTORS OF ACTIVITY THAT HAVE A NATURAL ALIGNMENT WITH SPEIK

There are some sectors of activity in which the nature of the work makes SPEIK particularly suitable for adaptation and dissemination.

Corporate Training Departments

Many large corporations and non-profits have substantial training departments whose mission is to ensure that employees have both the initial and follow-up training that keeps employees well-prepared for their jobs. These departments face some of the same challenges that educators face—keeping participants engaged, making appropriate adjustments based on the level of group comprehension, and documenting the level of learning gain for both individuals and groups. SPEIK technology is very helpful for these purposes, and for that reason, we expect that the use of SPEIK by corporate trainers—in-house or hired as contractors—will likely grow.

As this happens, there will be an opportunity for SPEIK to spread to other parts of the organization, but this will require companies to overcome barriers to cooperation. In both the corporate world and in educational settings, there can be an installed base of SPEIK systems that are being used only in classroom environments. Corporate trainers may not be thinking about how SPEIK might be used company-wide. However, they are in a position to form cooperative sharing arrangements that would allow the other parts of the company outside the training unit to benefit from using the technology.

Social Inclusion, Diversity, and Equity Specialists

Professionals who focus on these topics, including ourselves, do so largely because of a deeply held belief in the importance of making sure that all voices affected by a situation have a chance to equally and fairly contribute to decisions. People who have made this a focus of their lives typically are attracted to this field because, for whatever reason, they value countering the societal aversion to addressing deeply divisive and thorny topics. Lastly, people who do inclusion work are particularly attuned to the idea that differences in perceptions matter, and need to be examined honestly to create a society that is fair to everyone.

SPEIK can be a special ally to people in this field. Since the technology is commonly used in a way that people can anonymously submit their views, SPEIK has a special value when part of the challenge is to help people become more comfortable expressing views that they deeply hold but are less then fully comfortable expressing. When we have worked with people who specialize in this type of work, one of the most commonly cited advantages of the technology is its ability to elicit responses that may be more candid because they are registered as rapid anonymous responses.

If used well, the technology invites people to examine the relationship between identity, perception, and experience. The idea that there are powerful but often hidden connections between these realms is a core belief of most inclusion specialists. As we have discussed, the cross-tabulation feature can provide an almost unparalleled tool to demonstrate to skeptics that differences matter to both how people see the world and how the world sees them.

Al Jackson
Organizational Development Consultant

Mr. Jackson was a participant in a SPEIK opening session at a conference focused on diversity.

Love the technology for many reasons: one of them is what it does to let the audience feel less intimidated by what can be some very serious issues. As a diversity tool, it gives you a chance to be influential with people who might be open to data, to a process, but might not be open to you as a subject matter expert or as a person. If you are just talking by yourself, they may have reasons not to want to accept you. It obviously is the wave of the future.

Glenn Harris
Center for Social Inclusion, New York, New York

Mr. Harris used SPEIK devices very extensively when he headed the Seattle Department of Civil Rights and was often leading community meetings.

What are the devices useful for?

I think that devices are useful for three broad purposes. First, humor. Usually, I start things off with a ridiculous question. I used to do a lot of meetings in the most ethnically diverse zip code in the US, even though Seattle was one of the whitest cities. My first question was usually: which of these is your favorite type of chicken? The answers would include things like: curry chicken, abobo chicken, smothered chicken, and so on. People would overwhelmingly vote for what they grew up with. So the question was a way of starting the conversation about the diversity of the group and the diversity of the area. My schtick was always to look at the responses, acknowledge the vote, and then say, "That vote is nice, but everyone knows that fried chicken is really the best." Since I am visibly black, people would laugh at the ethnocentrism of that statement coming from a trainer and teacher of diversity and inclusion.

The second use is for sharing data. I used to do a lot of trainings, and people would much better remember a fact if I asked a question about it than if I just told them. We would often be trying to get people's heads around the reality of racial disparities. For instance, we would ask, "What is the ratio of tuberculosis of Asians to whites?"; the answers were something like; 3:1, 5:1, 10:1, 30:1, and 50:1. Very few people guessed the correct answer, which was something like 30:1. Sometimes you could hear the room gasp. People would not have remembered this if we just told them. The polling result also helped convey our message that disparities are not just a white/black thing. We would do this kind of thing for many stats, like infant mortality, home ownership, the chance of going to prison, and some others. Even people who were very aware of the idea of disparities were often very surprised, and remembered these facts, and the point behind teaching them.

The third way I use them is to reinforce concepts. I think that any exercise or process that you do in a small group you can do just as well or better in a big group using the

Glenn Harris, continued

technology. One of things I often do is to show people how we may have different definitions of the same thing, but might have common values underneath it. I might create different dilemmas, like polling them on different definitions of concepts as merit, or institutional racism, or asking how much they likely think it is that society will ever get rid of racism. My real point with the clickers is to confirm everyone in the room. People need to know that their opinion is okay, and that we can have different opinions about some important things and still work together.

Why do you think the devices are helpful?

I am a deep believer that adults learn from going through three steps: confirmation, contradiction, and continuity. Unlike kids, adults need to see have their views of a situation are confirmed. They need to be confirmed in where they currently stand. If you don't acknowledge where they are, they don't listen. Then, step 2 is that you have to offer them something new that they have not thought of, maybe even that goes against their old ideas. Then step 3 is you have to help them put the information into action. As adults, we have figured out that there is more information out there than we can hold. So if you cannot use it then you will not keep it. There is no point in it.

The clickers help you with all three steps in a meaningful way. They allow you to create a space of confirmation where people are already at. They allow you to introduce concepts in a way that is interactive and engaging. And then also allow you to get people thinking about next steps. We frequently use them to have people think about the future. We might say these are the five things that might happen next, choose which one you plan to do. Or we might say "there are four ways to apply this information; which will you do?".

The confirmation/contradiction/continuity sequence is an important model for all adult learning, but it is particularly important for difficult conversations, like those about race. As the tension increases in a conversation, those three steps become more essential. And, the three steps are least likely to happen. That's the nature of a fight: you skip over confirmation and continuity and go straight to contradiction.

Dialogue, Deliberation, and Democratic Practice Specialists

There is a small world-wide movement that emphasizes potential for improving civic life by fostering greater connection among communities and between communities and government. Organizations such as the International Association of Public Participation and the National Coalition of Dialogue and Deliberation in the United States are examples of this movement. Our sense is that the biggest impediment to these groups becoming sources of dissemination for SPEIK is something we mentioned earlier—that many practitioners are independent consultants who think that they cannot afford to make an investment in the technology.

Our experience is that people with this interest often have an intuitive appreciation for the various ways that SPEIK can help groups include more voices and have more effective conversations. In addition, the way that SPEIK promotes the idea of democratic values (more extensively discussed below), is also highly aligned with deeply held passions of people in the dialogue, deliberation, and democracy movements. For this reason, we will remain hopeful that at some point the institutional obstacles such as lack of sharing among practitioners) will be mounted and the technology's level of use will rise significantly.

Urban Planners and Others Whose Work Emphasizes Public Engagement

By the nature of their work, urban planners have an obligation that the public will play at least some role in the decisions they are supporting. In fact, the code of ethics of the American Planning Association states that "We shall give people the opportunity to have a meaningful impact on the development of plans and programs that may affect them." In theory, planners should be keen on methods of engaging people that increase the efficiency in the process of assessing public will.

In reality, the planning profession is progressing much slower than we think it should even in spreading basic facilitation skills that will help planners hear clearly from groups of people. This is not only a problem for planners; a similar situation exists with regard to similar professions that should care about input from members of the public, such as social workers and public policy professionals.

Although the sophistication in public engagement practice among planners and these other professionals is far less than it should be, there are some reasons to be optimistic. For instance, a few leading planning firms are beginning to recognize that more and better public input makes for fewer planning mistakes, and may even create a competitive edge. Nevertheless, the progress among urban planners is limited, which we find especially troubling because one of us (David) has a doctorate in the field.

Community Organizers

In theory, a primary task of a community organizer is to help groups of people affected by common problems to find their points of consensus and to unite behind a common strategy that will be collectively helpful. As we have discussed, SPEIK is well-suited for helping a group with these tasks. It bears noting that many community organizers would state that an important larger task of the organizer is to promote democratic decision-making. Much organizing work, many argue, is created because society structures its arrangements in ways that help some people and hurt others. Not only are organizers helping communities achieve short-term outcomes, but they are also inviting communities to re-think how decisions are made.

The idea that every voice should count and that it is vital to create processes to ensure that some voices do not dominate over others is one that most community organizers would heartily support and that is embodied by how the technology works. When we have exposed community organizers to the technology at conferences, they are particularly likely to express their enthusiasm about the possibilities.

Even though most people connected to the work of community organizers have emphasized the alignment between the technology and this work, others have seen possible tensions to contemplate.

Public Health and Youth Advocates

Advocates who work for organizations that promote public health and that focus on youth often have two important tasks when engaging groups of people. A primary task is disseminating information that will help them make better decisions. But an equally important task is eliciting information that can be used for program planning. The fact that SPEIK allows for anonymity greatly increases its value in helping program planners learn about

McCrae Parker
Senior Staff Person
Zero Divide

Mr. Parker helped his organization bring the latest technology to community organizers and other non-profit leaders.

In noticing the reaction of organizers to a demonstration, he indicated that, "One factor to consider is that this technology allows the community folk to speak directly about what they want. This may raise some challenges for organizers, who are used to serving as an intermediary between communities and funders. The organizer has to think about what happens if it turns out that what he wants to do for the community is not what the community wants. You now have gone from rumors that this might be the case to direct proof. And organizers get funded based on the idea that they speak for the community."

the prevalence of health-related behavior that people do not like to admit to. One executive director of a youth organization who has used the devices at large youth conclaves spoke to this point directly. As noted earlier in the book, many groups who need public health services often do not convey the realities of their lives in traditional meeting settings.

Conflict Resolution Specialists

While many specialists in conflict resolution focus on interpersonal disputes, a substantial portion of the work in this field focuses on conflict between groups—whether these groups are based on organizational affiliation, identity, or specific interests. We submit that conflict resolution (CR) specialists who work at the group level will eventually recognize that SPEIK is a useful tool.

This is largely because SPEIK can be used to increase empathy between people who, because they are entrenched in the current conflict, often have a tendency to regard their opponents as fundamentally different than themselves. As we have discussed, a sequence of polling questions can be designed to help establish the idea that everyone in the room is a part of a sub-group of those

Chirsty Zimani
Executive Director
Day One, Pasadena, California

Ms. Zimani has used the devices at large youth conclaves.

I think collecting that data really expressed the importance of having programs that we were delivering. And it made us understand what the kids are really dealing with, what we're up against, and where we need to focus our efforts. We learned how to fine-tune our programs to make access easier to the populations we're serving. And as what we learned also made it easier to advocate to the city. I think it helps us as a community identify weaknesses we can strengthen.

who are "like" themselves, whether this is because of hobbies, backgrounds, lifestyle, identity, or other factors. By strategically asking such questions and revealing answers in a savvy way—cross tabs can be relevant here—a CR professional can help undermine the empathy gap between folks on different sides of a conflict.

We have also discussed how SPEIK questions can be designed to help people see how identity, experiences, and perspective are related. This capacity is linked to a key strategy for CR specialists— namely, getting combatants to see the situation from other points of view. Further, the ability of a polling sequence to show people how those on opposing sides of a conflict might be harmed in a similar way by the unresolved conflict also makes it likely that SPEIK will eventually become a standard item in the toolkit of conflict resolution professionals who work on group conflict.

Public Officials (appointed and elected) and their Staffs

We have already discussed the advantages of SPEIK for professionals in agencies with a responsibility for hearing from the public, such as urban planning or public health. This same analysis applies to public officials (both elected and appointed) and their staffs. The savvy use of SPEIK could provide a very effective alternative to the way that such officials "listen" to people in public meetings today. Often, such sessions are organized around a sequence of people forming a queue to give their short speech. When the meeting is crowded because a controversy is brewing, either most of those gathered do not get to speak, or the meeting's conclusion is much later than anyone would call reasonable. The way that officials, attendees, and the media read the room to assess the feeling in the crowd—whose constitution is often demographically unrepresentative and reflects which special interest group did the best community mobilization—usually focuses on levels of non-verbal expression as applause, cheering, hissing, and the like.

It is not hard to envision public officials using SPEIK to hear what their constituents are thinking. (For an example, see the Barstow Desert Dispatch, August 27, 2014, City Hall Seeks Public Opinion). Questions could be constructed that might go across a wide span of issues. Or, if the official wanted to understand or educate the public on one issue area, the queries might be designed to explore some of the trade-offs and dilemmas embedded in the situation. No matter which approach was used, both the official, the public, and the media would contextualize the findings with precise knowledge about how close the gathering reflected the demography of relevant larger populations. Officials would have to decide how much they wanted to use these settings to take direction from their constituents versus to try to lead the public to their own way of thinking.

Although we are not aware of cases of candidates for office using SPEIK during campaign events, we can also imagine how a

---

Mala Nagarajan
Non-profit Consultant

Ms. Nagarajan saw a demonstration of SPEIK at a conference of non-profit leaders.

I can really see coalitions and community organizers using this. It would allow the organizers to get voices that would not typically be raised. There are a few powerful voices in any coalition or large organization and then there are a lot of voices that typically are not heard and, with technology like this, you can get a much better pulse of the whole group that there's no way to do right now.

candidate for office might use SPEIK for this purpose. This might be particularly fruitful when a candidate's "brand" includes being a force for civility, empathy, while maintaining principles. A campaign might create events where the crowd was constructed to include a portion of people of undecided voters who disagree with the candidate on some issues. By engaging the group on different issues, the candidate could bolster his or her standing as one who is capable of hearing opposing views, but is still able to maintain an attitude of respect and broadmindedness.

Candidate debates seem a potentially fruitful place to use the technology. Typically, these forums have large studio audiences, but often, they are highly discouraged from even non-verbal responses that express their feelings. This seems a colossal waste of the presence of people. We envision candidate forums designed with the exact opposite imperative—why not make the debates more electric by designing them around the candidates' responses to the expressed perspective of the citizens gathered?

Capacity-Building Professionals

Groups that consider themselves focused on improving the ability of non-profit companies or social enterprise groups are sometimes called the "capacity builders". These include non-profit associations, some consulting firms, organizations dedicated to improved governance, and a substantial portion of the foundation community. In the non-profit world, there are also organizations that are well positioned to foster the spread of SPEIK. Groups doing this work often portray themselves as mission-level commitment to spreading the use of organizational practices that are inclusive and democratic.

In our opinion, there are several reasons that such entities are well positioned to positively influence the trend toward greater audience participation. First, the mission of many of these groups is to strengthen the ability of non-profit organizations to make good decisions, and to connect better to their constituent communities. Audience polling is a good tool for each of these goals.

A primary reason that capacity building organizations and many philanthropies exist is to support the operation of many groups; as such, they sometimes operate as hubs of capacity building within a loose network of organizations. In addition, capacity-building organizations have larger budgets than many of the organizations they are trying to support; they can often more easily handle investing in new technology. They also have the ability to see trends emerging and to incentivize changes in behavior or practices by the organizations they are charged to assist. Capacity-building groups could acquire the technology and follow-up technical assistance, and make SPEIK available to groups they support which might individually have meetings only on an occasional basis.

Finally, many capacity-building organizations and philanthropy also have something of a populist mission, in that they are dedicated to counter power arrangements where elites tend to dominate group decision-making. Accordingly, capacity building organizations should find a natural resonance with the way that SPEIK highlights the equal value of every voice.

In the final chapter, we will continue the discussion of values that tend to be re-enforced by the technology. As we will see, SPEIK both reflects and promotes some specific values, even if sponsors and presenters do not talk about these values directly. While these values are undoubtedly positive, promoting them to their meeting participants may put sponsors in a position to take on some complexities, and perhaps some risks. Participants may expect sponsors to subsequently uphold these values, perhaps past the point where the sponsor thinks it is most useful to do so. If these participants are stakeholders who matter, such a situation may create some tensions. It could be that this dynamic of increasing accountability to stakeholders for the underlying values of SPEIK may slow down the dissemination of the technology.

7.

TOWARDS
GREATER
CLARITY

7

Clarity

It is worth briefly restating some of the core dynamics that make SPEIK effective, before we lay out our thoughts about the larger implications of the technology beyond efficacy in the moment.

- Many meetings are largely pre-scripted events where the attendees are primarily observing the meeting, not directly contributing to it. By using SPEIK simply for entertainment, meeting conveners (defined as meeting strategists, sponsors, and presenters working collaboratively) can make meetings more engaging and fun, partly because gatherings will have an element that is at least slightly unpredictable.
- If the conveners go beyond using SPEIK as an entertaining engagement tool and link its use to strategic objectives, the participants will create information that is useful for some relevant decisions.
- The value of SPEIK queries to an organization's decisions depends on the questions that are posed to the participants, the answers given, and perhaps most importantly, how the sponsor regards their relationship to the participants. A useful way to think about the continuum of sponsor/ participant relationships that are embodied in polling questions is as follows:

> ## RELATIONSHIP CONTINUUM:
>
> **CONSUMERS** Sponsors care about polling results because the answers (and the polling process itself) help conveners deliver a better experience to the meeting consumers in the moment.
>
> **CUSTOMERS** Customers care about polling results because the answers will help the sponsor fine-tune the relationship with them that extends beyond the meeting.
>
> **COUNSELORS** Sponsors care about polling results because the sponsor wants considered advice about decisions that the sponsor will make.
>
> **COLLABORATORS** Sponsors care about polling because it helps the sponsor set the tone for activity that is best thought of as an on-going partnership with the participants.

- The use of the technology requires the formulation of polling questions that are engaging to the participants and useful to the sponsor. Developing these questions pushes the meeting strategist and the sponsor to think more clearly about their desired outcome of each meeting moment when SPEIK might be used.
- The meeting moments to which SPEIK can add value can be thought of as focusing on accomplishing one or more of the following goals:

- Download—conveying information to participants;
- Feedback—eliciting information directly from participants; and
- Crosstalk—fostering exchanges between participants that will advance their thinking.

It is important to note that the distinctions between types of participants relationships and between meeting modes is not hard and fast; in an actual gathering, meeting moments and the SPEIK questions that enliven them merge into each other. In addition, these dynamics can also vary through the course of a convening.[1].

SPEIK is a powerful tool that can be used to facilitate new approaches to group decision-making. Its capacity to quickly and accurately assess the perspective of a group of stakeholders offers new possibilities for group decision-making. Before SPEIK, it was not possible to, for example, create a gathering of hundreds of company employees (or some sizeable subset of them) and easily get their perspective on the company's newly proposed policies, for example, work-from-home, dress code, or on new strategic initiatives. It was not possible for a city's mayor to gather a representative sample of constituents of the city (or subset of it) and obtain valuable detailed feedback on a wide range of proposals and initiatives, such as a draft city budget or a new master plan. A university president could not call hundreds of faculty, staff, and students together—in one meeting or in separate meetings—and get their collective response to a new proposal for addressing hate speech, or on plans for a

---

[1] Imagine a daylong meeting of a statewide professional association of professional planners. One could easily imagine a moment when conveners use SPEIK to confirm that the participants (as meeting consumers) retained the download of a key fact about the organization's budget deficit, and another moment when conveners ask the group for feedback on how they regarded the monthly newsletter (as customers). At a different point, the conveners might be using SPEIK to encourage the attendees to a dialogue that distills their collective advice (as counselors) about the pros and cons of a proposed collaboration with another organization; finally, the day might end with the conveners letting the membership choose (as collaborators) its annual holiday volunteer project, which might be decided by majority rule.

campus expansion paid for by raised fees and budget cuts. All of these gatherings are now possible and can produce information that can be used immediately.

For a very long time, people have debated the respective roles of leaders and group members as they make decisions and take collective action. People have also argued about whose input should be included on different types of decisions. Now that SPEIK exists, a leader of a group can get feedback on any number of issues from scores, hundreds, or thousands of stakeholders, and do so in a process that is not itself burdensome. Leaders just need to decide which issues it wants input on, decide the size of the group and stakeholders which need to be included, and design the meeting so that the group is sufficiently well-informed and can weigh in. With SPEIK, leaders of all types can easily know with great precision what various stakeholders think. This is new, and creates significant opportunities and profound new questions.

We've outlined numerous situations in which SPEIK can be of benefit. But the questions abound: What are the potential benefits, risks and downsides from using polling as a strategic tool for engaging stakeholders? And what are the specific conditions under which polling participants should or should not take place? When should leaders consult with—or perhaps rely on—group wisdom, and when should leaders keep their own counsel and not solicit feedback from stakeholders? When do stakeholders—or specific subsets of them—perceive the solicitation of their feedback as a burden? When does asking for input from stakeholder groups introduce disorder into the decision-making process, shake group confidence, foster unproductive group think and/or lead to bad decisions?

We will not herein attempt to answer those questions. It is rather early for that—SPEIK is yet to have a significant impact on the meeting market and on organizational decision-making. While it is far too early to try to answer those questions, it is not too early to raise them. Specifically, we want to raise the question of values, since like any other technology, SPEIK is not value free. We must ask:

Q. What are the values that are embodied by SPEIK?

Q. What additional work, is required, if any, by conveners if they are to appropriately account for these values?

Q. How might we start thinking about the upsides and downsides of the technology and these attendant complexities about values?

The values and issues that SPEIK raises and that we will explore include:

- Inclusion and equality,
- The significance of physical presence at meetings,
- The definition of meaningful participation,
- Transparency and accountability, and
- Group wisdom and its relationship to democratic principles.

Each of these ideas tends to generate support on the surface. But where decisions need to be made in a reasonably efficient manner, employing a process that embraces these values can create dilemmas, and perhaps sources of contention. Moreover, organizations that use SPEIK in order to advance their objectives potentially make themselves subject to scrutiny regarding the degree to which they are living up to the underlying values that SPEIK is promoting. While we think that the upside benefit is greater than the downside, it is critical that people who play all roles in organizational and community decisions think through these values and the trade-offs that come with them.

Inclusion and Equality (Whose voice counts?)

SPEIK reinforces the idea that each person's contribution to the group is important, and that each person's perspective matters equally. As a general proposition, the idea that each person's contribution matters is widely supported, at least in western democracies, and has been for centuries.

As a practical matter however, this value, like most values, exists in tension with other considerations. This is particularly true regarding the idea that all voices should matter equally. In decisions that affect groups, a common conundrum is whether some voices should count more than others because of the differential impact of the decision, different levels of knowledge, or other factors. Even when the groups are relatively small—like a large family choosing where and when to have a reunion—the degree of relative weight to give to some opinions over others can become a point of contention. What happens when people disagree about the importance of inclusion and equality in settings?

For instance, several years ago, a foundation executive (let's call this person "Pat") was on a planning committee that was preparing for a national conference of managers in philanthropy. She had worked to make it possible for a plenary session to include the use of audience polling. SPEIK was expected to help the conference clarify the upcoming central challenges the foundation community was facing. The meeting would include a broad range of participants, from junior program officers at small foundations to the board chairperson of one of the largest philanthropic organizations in the country. The goal of the session was to give guidance to the association behind the conference about their priorities to help the sector.

According to Pat, during the planning discussions, some members of the planning team repeatedly questioned whether there was a way to put different weights on attendees' votes. It turned out that this was not possible at the time. Though the planning committee used SPEIK at the conference anyway, Pat thought these conversations were noteworthy, especially because everyone on the planning team portrayed themselves and their respective organizations as having a strong commitment to democratic values, especially inclusion and equality.

Even if such concerns seem less valid for a session with several hundred people giving general guidance than for other types of meetings, the issue of whose voice counts and how much will be one that conveners will have to think through. We expect that meeting sponsors who use SPEIK will come under scrutiny about whether they are being sufficiently inclusive and giving the proper weight to stakeholders of different types. In our experience, this is most likely when participants are told that they are being engaged as counselors or collaborators.

The reader will recall the meetings on Ground Zero and New Orleans recovery mentioned earlier. In each of these cases, a critical meeting success factor for both the sponsor and the public was the representiveness of the gathering. In each case, the meeting strategist had to persuade the sponsor to allocate a substantial portion of the budget so that scores of outreach workers could be hired to produce sufficient demographic diversity at the meeting. Subsequently, these contractors had to be deftly and diligently managed to ensure performance.

The fact that there might be contention and/or consternation about inclusion and equality during group processes is not because of the use of SPEIK. Throughout history, people have commonly raised concerns about whose voices are included when group decision-making is undertaken. However, when sponsors use SPEIK, they are promoting the idea that relevant groups should be included, as well as making a statement about whose perspectives matter. More importantly, SPEIK makes it possible to know—in real-time and with precision—who is actually at the table and who is not.

The significance of physical presence at meetings (Who needs to be there?)

SPEIK's fundamental power is in quickly and efficiently helping the group see the diversity of its perspectives. To the extent that SPEIK focuses group attention on the interplay of participants input on polling questions, SPEIK arguably has a somewhat reductionist aspect. On its own and without a broader context, the primacy of the diversity and interplay of submitted views suggests that a person's contribution to a meeting is significantly embodied in whatever input they make through the SPEIK device.

Currently, there are several SPEIK systems that allow people who are not in the room but who are connected via the Internet to register their vote on questions before the group. Over time, as internet connections improve and commuting costs rise, people who plan meetings may be motivated by a number of factors to more critically examine their need for people to be physically present at a meeting, (e.g. increased sophistication of remote communications systems, rise in commuting costs). And it is reasonable for participants to wonder why they should attend a meeting if they can receive information and/or effectively provide feedback from a remote location.

Some SPEIK systems can currently link remote participants to a meeting and obtain their feedback, but most cannot. Recall Kerry Wade (p. 112), the neighborhood outreach specialist who uses SPEIK extensively. She favorably anticipates doing her neighborhood health assessment meetings with app-based SPEIK systems so that the meetings can include people who want desperately to participate in public meetings but who cannot attend them. Over time, we expect that people who cannot come to meetings will increasingly be able to not just virtually attend the meeting, but also to participate in the polling while it is happening. (This technology already exists. Twice each year, Ms. Wade lends her SPEIK expertise to a public affairs television show, Seattle Speaks, that integrates the polling of both the studio audience and home viewers into the meeting.)

But one must pose the question: does having participants share physical space in a meeting in some way influence its outcome in a way that is meaningful? Put differently, what are the special things that happen from people being in the same physical space during a meeting? Is it the conversation when not polling? Is there something special about sharing physical space that augments a meeting?

Though we have trouble naming it with precision, we think that there is something very special that can happen at a human level if the people are physically present at meetings and the environment is managed well. On the other hand, there may be times when a meeting is enhanced by the participation of a set of people who simply cannot be there. In our view, meeting strategists should always ask themselves if the meeting is producing a result that could not happen if the gathering was on-line. Clarity about meeting purpose is key, and discerning the degree to which a meeting is in download, feedback, or crosstalk mode may shed light on the question.

Given the increasing expense of in-person meetings and the greater ability of people to appear to each other virtually, we think that meeting strategists who want to make SPEIK a regular part of their toolbox will face pressures that go in opposite directions. On the one hand, it will be important to provide ways for people who cannot attend meetings to be able to add their contribution. On the other hand, to the extent that a strategist thinks that physical presence at the meeting improves the experience or makes it possible to generate better information, it will be important to create in-the-room processes that add value for the participants. In addition to executing meeting design strategies that create more satisfaction for those who attend, the strategist will also need to learn how meeting value is best presented to participants so they will get the combination of in-person and virtual participation that leads to the best results.

Meaningful Participation (What do people have to know to weigh in?)

SPEIK also promotes the idea of meaningful participation, namely, that the participants will be educated through the process in order to rationally weigh in on issues put in front of them. Further, the idea of meaningful participation suggests that these participant materials will be created in an unbiased manner and be of sufficient quality to improve understanding.

Meeting strategists routinely think about the best strategies for introducing content to meeting attendees. But SPEIK does create new challenges in this regard—specifically, SPEIK can be deployed to verify how well-prepared participants feel for continuing to engage the topic. Comprehension and participant readiness of deliberation can both be explicitly checked. This is particularly important in a meeting where the participants are regarded as counselors or collaborators. In these instances, the quality of the process and materials used to engage the participants is a critical success factor for the meeting, so it may make sense to verify that people feel ready to weigh in on the issues.

The closer the participants' role is to the collaborator end of the spectrum, the more complex it is to make sure they are ready to give advice or make decisions. In preparing materials for such meetings, the meeting strategist must consider a variety of questions, such as:

1. What are the aspects of the issues that it makes sense to get input on?

2. What is the knowledge level of the participants before the meeting?

3. What is the information that will enhance their engagement and that will be perceived as unbiased by people with very different points of view?

4. What should be the role of presentation, reading, or discussion in putting participants in positions to weigh in meaningfully?

5. Are there historical or emotional factors that, if not addressed, will keep people from engaging? Similarly, are there factors that may be relevant but, if raised, will undermine engagement? (Recall the suggested avoiding of the race topic by participants in the New Orleans meeting.)

6. How much discussion, if any, is needed before participants can weigh in on the topic? Does this discussion need to be facilitated to be effective?

7. If reviewing materials are distributed in advance, how much participant motivation can be expected? Should incentives, of some sort, be offered to support greater engagement?

One could argue that all of these questions are ones that are typically addressed by a skillful meeting strategist. However, the significance of answering these questions well or poorly matters much more for high-input meetings using SPEIK. If a meeting strategist is off the mark in answering these questions and designs a low-input traditional meeting, the most likely worst case scenario is that many people leave the meeting feeling that the meeting was a waste of their time and that they attended a poorly run dog and pony show. By contrast, if the strategist gets these questions wrong and designs a high-input meeting using SPEIK on that basis, people will leave with a much higher level of frustration, since they had been led to think they would be involved in a process that was coherent enough so that their input could matter.

In using SPEIK to engage participants, meeting strategists subject themselves to pressures about the thoroughness and accuracy of whatever process will be used to prepare participants to engage; in addition, meeting participants will also examine whether the materials used to engage them are biased. SPEIK is emerging at a time when people are used to frequent attempts to manipulate them by omnipresent media. Further, many people are skeptical that a sponsor really wants to get feedback for decision-making. Both of these factors combine to often create a great deal of skepticism about whether the meeting is designed to manufacture consent to positions the sponsor already has taken. This is particularly true if the underlying subject is contentious, or if people feel that the meeting sponsor is already leaning in a specific direction.

As a result, it is critical that sufficient care be taken and expertise applied to remove bias from processes and materials designed to prepare participants to engage topics. Our sense is that doing the meeting design work to deeply engage participants and avoid perceptions of bias is more time consuming than creating the pre-scripted observational events where participants have minimal input. To put it plainly: designing a meeting based on a sponsor hearing from participants is harder than creating one that allows a sponsor to just talk to them. But, in our opinion, the sponsor and the participants will get more out of a well-structured and inclusive exchange. Sponsors and strategists who design meetings based on hearing from people subject themselves to additional pressures— even though they are designing the meeting around getting feedback on substance, they will likely receive some feedback on the process, whether they ask for it or not. Participation tends to empower people.

Transparency and Accountability (Can the results be trusted?)

SPEIK systems tend to promote the value of transparency, which is sometimes defined as openness, clarity, and lack of bias. Many meeting strategists exposed to SPEIK are excited about it because of their perception that it creates results that are unfiltered: a question is asked, people only have a few seconds to respond, results are quickly generated. The speed of this process itself conveys to people that neither the participants nor the conveners are editing or filtering the results.

Along the same lines, we have heard other meeting strategists positively comment about the way SPEIK tends to foster deeply honest interactions and sharing between people and institutions. Conceivably, one way for public agencies (and maybe non-public organizations) to get more feedback from their constituents is to create meetings that are designed to be engaging, fun, educational, and offer opportunities to provide feedback. Such meetings may represent a new model for engaging the public and collecting usable data. Given the difficulties of getting people to complete on-line surveys because of language barriers, internet access constraints, and other factors, sponsors might assess whether they might get more information from communities by widely deploying this emergent model.

As they make this assessment, one factor that they are likely to start considering is the attendant risks of creating settings where polling technology is publicly used. When surveys are done individually (on paper or on-line), the organization doing the survey can always make the results hard to access. By contrast, when SPEIK is publicly deployed and the results are displayed in order to engage people, those participants know that the results are available. Once an organization shows a willingness to display results by doing surveys publicly, it may face increased interest from the stakeholders in the results of other surveys, even ones done in other ways.

There are other dilemmas that may be created by using SPEIK, especially in complex organizational systems. What if the answers to a survey question have the potential to embarrass the meeting sponsor, or the sponsor's allies? Should the sponsor anticipate such problems and steer away from such questions? Should a polling facilitator refuse requests to display some data if the participants want to see it? What dynamics do such decisions create with respect to stakeholder skepticism about the process?

Just as a sponsor's decision to engage people in a public survey subjects them to pressure to display results, asking people for their perspective creates expectations that their input will have some type of impact.[2] This is true of on-line surveys and even more so with ones that might be done publicly. When a sponsor asks for information, people will assume that this is not just a solitary action, but part of a sequence of actions that includes sharing the results and acting upon them. Sponsors who contemplate leveraging the advantages of SPEIK should be aware of the transparency and accountability that participants often think are embedded in the process.

Democracy and Group Wisdom (Who decides?)

The initial and perhaps most important value promoted by SPEIK is that there is important wisdom to be had from examining the diverse perspectives and collective preferences of a group. The idea that a group of people will, if equipped with unbiased information and a chance to meaningfully consider possibilities, choose courses of actions that are best for it is a core principle of democratic governance. Beyond the realm of politics, the idea that there can be great wisdom in the amalgamation of perspectives in a group is increasingly recognized, researched, and documented.

But we recognize that this has its limits and that the collective brain is not always correct. To take examples from the past, many historians estimate that before the American Revolutionary War, public opinion among colonialists was equally divided among those in favor of, against, and neutral about breaking away from England. Those who feel the Revolutionary War was a positive thing are

---

[2] "One of the worst things I have seen for trust and morale is to ask for employee input year after year and never do anything in response to it," says Ellyn McKay of CEO Vision, a Washington, DC area organizational coaching firm. "You create a worse result than just not asking for this information at all. "

pleased that the decision to revolt was not taken through public opinion polls or put to a vote. To highlight another example, if public opinion polls or votes were taken in the South of the 1960's about the passage of national civil rights legislation, it would have likely lost by an overwhelming landslide. Sometimes, what groups need for their long-run best interests is an effective mechanism to counter the tyranny of the majority.

In general, we believe that leaders tapping into the collective brain leads to good results. But we recognize that this is just a generalization. As the above examples illustrate, there are times when the mob is just a mob and leaders must lead. But there are other times when the mob is smart, logical, and considers a wide array of relevant factors more effectively than a leader and a small number of top advisors.

SPEIK is an excellent tool for distilling the mindset of the group; its core features comprise three of the four characteristics of "wise crowds.[3] But who gets to decide which crowd can be entrusted with leading decision-making on a specific issue? And how does the ease and availability of SPEIK affect how these questions are considered?

These are not just theoretical questions, but are apropos across a spectrum of organizational life. Here are five very different examples of settings in which these issues might come up, and accompanying questions that illustrate what leaders may face as SPEIK is increasingly disseminated through society.

---

[3] In *The Wisdom on Crowds*, James Suroweicki describes four elements that are needed for a group to access its collective wisdom: 1) Diversity of opinion: Each person should have private information even if it is just an eccentric interpretation of the known facts, 2) Independence: People's opinions are not determined by the opinions of those around them, 3) Decentalization: People are able to specialize and draw on local knowledge, and 4) Aggregation: Some mechanism exists for turning private judgments into a collective. SPEIK by its core nature is to aggregate opinion, thus comprising characteristic #4; it facilitates independence (#3), by encouraging people to express their views privately, anonymously, and simultaneously; SPEIK also is designed to both support and allow the assessment of diversity in the room (#1). Arguably, SPEIK is a primary agent for helping a crowd become wise.

- What are the circumstances when foundations should take direction from their grantees?
- When should community organizers stop working to further educate a group and put strategic or tactical issues up for a neighborhood vote?
- How often should a mayor convene a city-wide or district-wide summit so the people can weigh in on current decisions?
- When should the CEO of a mid-size company look for guidance from its senior management? From its sales team? From its entire set of employees?
- When should a university president solicit the perspectives of faculty, staff, and students?

Leaders of a system vary on how much feedback they are willing to accept from groups they oversee. It is also true that leaders, even the most flexible and open-minded, need to decide when and how much feedback is appropriate. SPEIK makes the process of group feedback easier, but framing questions for groups and getting their feedback is still a messy and time-consuming process, compared to simply making decisions based on more traditional and less inclusive means of getting input. (These traditional methods might include "listening sessions" that might be attended by 300 people but where only a few get to say anything).

What must be considered is the fact that once leaders use SPEIK to get feedback on certain issues, some sub-groups in the system may begin to raise questions about why the technology is not used for an assortment of other decisions. For example, what if middle managers who have been engaged using SPEIK to weigh in on quality management processes subsequently decide that top management should consider their views on other topics, like the location of the next holiday party, the level of company morale, or the recent performance of a long-term supplier? Even if the leaders choose to not put such issues to the group, it is possible that someone might use Twitter or similar social media to push a poll out to some employees anyway.

(We have had some clients demur from convening stakeholders because of fears of what might happen from polling they cannot fully control. Several years ago, we worked with a university client who wanted to use SPEIK and other processes to get community input on a campus expansion plan. They were facing significant opposition from the community about their "land grab", and thought that they could reduce opposition and improve relations if they constructed an inclusive input process for deciding the mix of uses for the land they were about to acquire. After several initial meetings where we explained how our meeting would adapt to data in the room, they realized how easy it would be to create questions on the fly. They decided to not have public meetings because they feared that activists might pressure us to create new questions about whether the development should go forward or not, and they did not want to create new pressures on themselves.)

If meeting sponsors begin to engage some participants as customers as opposed to consumers, the sponsors will be sending a message that the collective preferences of the participants matters and that they want the group to significantly influence decision-making. Some participants may then conclude that they should be consulted as customers on other issues; they might think that they should be considered as counselors or even collaborators on some topics.

The phenomenon of leaders thinking their circle of advisors is broad enough and people outside that circle disagreeing is not new, and is, perhaps, an inevitable part of the dynamics of systems of any size and complexity. Power hierarchies are not new. Disagreements over who should be at the table of influence are not new. Certainly SPEIK does not create these dilemmas. However, the existence of SPEIK may bring related tensions into higher relief.

As leaders decide to engage SPEIK to leverage the advantages of group wisdom, the process of influencing decisions becomes more transparent to the entire system. SPEIK's existence in a system makes it easy to see what are the issues on which the leaders are subject to the influence of specific sub-groups. Everyone will know the issues on which leaders want to hear participants' voice, and when group opinion has limited impact. It will become clearer on what issues the leader views various stakeholders as customers, counselors, and collaborators, or as people who do not need to contribute directly to group decision-making. People may disagree—and scholars may someday study—whether transparency of such power dynamics is better for organizations or not.

Despite the cautions and caveats we have articulated in the last several pages, we remain deeply committed to spreading the use of SPEIK. We know that there will be times when a group's decisions will not be enhanced by more feedback, when leaders will use SPEIK disingenuously, and when feelings might be hurt because how SPEIK is used will let people know that they have little influence over issues on which they think they should have more voice. Nevertheless, we think that as a general proposition, giving participants more voice in meetings leads to better results, and that institutions and communities will we better off if the technology is used more than it is now.

We deeply believe that something special can happen in a meeting (and in a system) when people know that there are multiple chances for their voices to be heard, and when the group is consciously and transparently wrestling with the implications of its collective view. We each have seen many cases in which people who came into a SPEIK-enabled meeting as strangers preparing for combat felt the need to hug each other before leaving. When this happens, it is a recognition that something like a communion has happened, and part of the reason for this communion is that SPEIK helps people see themselves and others as part of a larger system.

Our deep belief is that people, organizations, and society will better address their problems if our meetings can help us see ourselves, others, and the structures in which we are situated with greater complexity, clarity, and interrelatedness. With SPEIK, a group can easily distill its collective wisdom and discern its group will based on the preferences of everyone in it. Our hope is that meetings start using this revolutionary capacity so that organizations, communities and society as a whole can do better at confronting problems and creating the future that people want.

Afterword
From Here to Ubiquity

In writing this book we have tried to balance our impulse to sermonize about the benefits of SPEIK and our wish to provide a clear explanation of how to obtain these benefits. Our intention was to reach people who might be converted and join the too slowly moving bandwagon toward group interactivity and participation as a standing expectation. As we close the book, we want to more fully embrace our belief that not only do we advocate the use of SPEIK to improve a variety of meetings, but we also seek to increase consumer awareness of the benefits of SPEIK and thus encourage people to take steps to help the technology spread. If we have persuaded you to join the effort to make interactivy a norm, what should you do?

We will examine this question by looking at the three major roles in a meeting—presenters, sponsors, and participants—and saying a little about some strategies that people in each of these roles might take to usher in a new approach to meetings.

Presenters

A significant obstacle for meeting professionals—speakers, conference planners, and workshop facilitators—is that becoming equipped to use SPEIK entails a separate effort to build new internal capacity. This obstacle may be particularly daunting for consultants like us who work in small independent firms. Building capacity requires time and money. Many meeting professionals do not have the volume of engagements to realize a fast return on investment. However, there are ways to overcome this hurdle.

For instance, meeting professionals can band together to share SPEIK interconnected systems, whether they be standalone devices or subscriptions to internet/cell phone-based systems. If professionals join forces in informal collectives to share the devices, the cost per person and the cost per use declines and becomes affordable. Similarly, such collectives could share the cost of trainers who might build each member's capacity to use the systems. Most importantly, such a collective could operate as a learning community that meets electronically after each use so that lessons are shared. And because the devices have gotten smaller (when standalone devices are used), such collectives could exist across distances, with the devices being shipped as needed.

Sponsors

Clearly, meeting sponsors are in a better position to promote the use of SPEIK. If meeting sponsors start asking meeting professionals who are not SPEIK-capable about the potential use of the technology, meeting professionals who want to maintain a competitive edge will probably start examining it.

Right now, there is very limited penetration in the meetings market for polling; someone who deploys polling in a way that is minimally competent so that the meeting objectives are enhanced will likely be experienced as bringing something very special to the table. As SPEIK technology becomes more widespread, sponsors will see it less as a cool toy and more as a meeting productivity tool; as a result, they are going to demand higher quality SPEIK experiences for their meetings. Even today, sponsors should start asking meeting professionals how they view the benefits and risks of greater interactivity at their meeting.

Participants

Even though their power is less than that of meeting sponsors, meeting participants have some ability to advance the trend toward greater interactivity forward. Meeting participants might consider raising the question of interactivity during meetings. Frequently, there are moments when it is clear that if there were a method of asking a group a question and instantly seeing the collective response, the objectives of the meeting would be advanced. Imagine what would happen if participants started letting facilitators know they believe that there is an easy-to-use technology that might be helpful to the group in navigating the moment that just occurred. In a public meeting, this might be done in front of the entire gathering. If presenters occasionally hear meeting participants suggest to them that it might improve their practice by adding a capacity that would help this meeting we are in right now, it will not be long before they themselves become more curious about SPEIK technology.

Event Planners, Venue Managers, and Meeting Support Specialists

If you work in the meetings industry as an event planner, venue manager, or audio-visual specialist, and you are interested in SPEIK, you have a dilemma. On the one hand, becoming proficient with the technology will allow you to add significant value to your clients or to your organization, because you will be able to create a special level of electricity that is very difficult to get in other ways. On the other hand, some peers and superiors may tell you that SPEIK is an aspect of meetings that is out of your lane.

Both of these ideas are true. SPEIK technology is something that is reasonably the province of any meeting professional; at the same time, any meeting professional can argue that thinking about whether and how to add the complexity of polling to a meeting is something that is someone else's job.

It is not clear in whose lap audience polling will fall in the long-run evolution of the technology. For now, this does not really matter. It is best to think of SPEIK as a technology that will likely grow; if you promote it, you are serving as a leader of a coming wave of innovation. The critical keys to helping this innovation take root are finding allies and creating initial successes. Given that SPEIK can help meetings in so many different ways—from making them more entertaining, to helping conveners better pursue existing objectives, to helping conveners by making progress on objectives that were not initially in play—the key to success is to chose which approach most inspires you and works best in the settings of the meetings you are connected to.

Even though increasing numbers of people have seen the technology, it is still relatively new, so initial success is important.

The deployment of polling needs to not just work technically, it needs to work well in the meeting, which means the questions must be designed well. It is best to find one to two other people who will help you introduce polling to your meeting, or to your organization. SPEIK works best when more than one person is thinking through how to meld it best with meeting objectives, presenters, and the mood of the group.

To find those allies in your organization or in others, it may be necessary to have a few people find some YouTube videos (including ones we have made) that explain the technology, and see who resonates with the possibilities. We have found that many people cannot comprehend how SPEIK can add value to a setting until they experience it first hand. It may be possible, to arrange a demonstration with a SPEIK company. Alternatively, it also may be possible to create a demonstration yourself, since some of the cell phone based SPEIK companies have free accounts that appear designed to help people become oriented to the technology.

Besides finding allies, the most important thing is to do everything possible to make sure your first venture is a success. When you try it for the first time, it is likely useful to tell people you are conducting a trial of an innovation, which helps people become more forgiving. And, of course, do not neglect to ask for feedback on the process.

THE ROLE OF RESEARCHERS

Looking at the far horizon of how meetings may evolve, it bears mentioning that academics play a role as well. At this point, we do think that there is a fair amount of good research that helps explain why polling technology is transformative, but the vast majority of this research is focused on the academic environment. Throughout this book, we have provided a few references from this growing body of literature; we see that many of the findings about audience polling in the classroom coincide with our experience about audience interactivity in the non-educational meeting setting. Our hope is that over time, educational psychologists, organizational development specialists, peace and conflict scholars, civic deliberation experts, and others concerned with fostering greater group learning, cooperation and similar positive goals will engage in robust research about these devices.

Readers who are interested in staying connected to others who have an interest in SPEIK systems should explore the following web locations:
- Web page for this book: www.read-the-room.com
- The Linked-In community involved in SPEIK is titled: Audience Response System Online Community

ABOUT THE AUTHORS

Dr. David Campt has provided consultation on engaging groups of people around issues important to them for more than 20 years. After attaining his doctorate from UC Berkeley in City Planning, he became a senior policy advisor with the President's Initiative on Race, where he was responsible for identifying promising practices in race relations and organizing dialogue efforts on behalf of President Bill Clinton.

Throughout his career, he has helped groups focus on a variety of topics including strategic planning, conflict resolution, creating more inclusive decision-making, leadership succession, cultural competence, and many others. His clients have varied widely, and have included the United States military (Navy and Coast Guard), large corporations, international organizations, foundations, federal, state, and local governments, universities, national associations, and large and small non-profit groups (such as AARP, American Federation of State, County and Municipal Employees, the YMCA, and the Western Justice Center). He has designed and facilitated discussions ranging from multi-day retreats for small groups to large-scale summits involving thousands of people.

This is his second book-length attempt to convey his insights about the keys to having more productive interpersonal interaction. His first book, *The Little Book of Dialogue for Difficult Subjects* (with Lisa Schirch, 2007), provides practical guidance about how individuals and organizations can use skills of dialogue to better solve shared challenges.

David is considered a national expert on issues of diversity, inclusion, and social equity. He does much of his consulting on inclusive decision-making and stakeholder engagement through The DWC Group: Dialogue. Wisdom. Collaboration. In his spare time, David is an avid skier and snowboarder. He has recently taken up rollerblading as a non-winter activity for going fast.

DAVID CAMPT
The DWC Group: Dialogue. Wisdom. Collaboration.
www.thedwcgroup.com
david@thedwcgroup.com

Matthew Freeman is a facilitator and trainer with over 10 years of experience working on race and diversity issues, civic engagement, and organizational development. Matthew has worked with a diverse roster of clients, from small non-profits to Fortune 500's companies, including Wells Fargo, Genworth, the German Marshall Fund, Virginia Commonwealth University, and the City of Richmond, Virginia. His projects have included facilitating dialogues with Members of Congress on the lingering impact of race in American society, and designing peer-learning exchanges between American and German cities.

Matthew was among the group of elite facilitators selected to teach a course on dialogue at an International Peace Builder's conference in Caux, Switzerland. Matthew is president of TMI Consulting of Richmond, Virginia.

When he is not working or listening to British rap, he is likely on his bike or getting knocked off of it by cars, trucks, or giant logs.

MATTHEW FREEMAN
TMI Consulting
www.tmiconsultinginc.com
matthew@tmiconsultinginc.com

BIBLIOGRAPHY

Banks, D. A. (Ed.). (2006). Audience response systems in higher education: Applications and cases. Hershey: Information Science Publishing.

Bohm, D. (1996). On dialogue. New York: Routledge.

Bruff, D. (2009). Teaching with classroom response systems: Creating active learning environments. San Francisco: Jossey-Bass.

Burnstein, R. A., and Lederman, L. M. (2001). Using wireless keypads in lecture classes. The Physics Teacher, 39 (1), 8–11.

Burton, K. (2006). The trial of an audience response system to facilitate problem-based learning in legal education. In D. A. Banks (Ed.), Audience response systems in higher education (pp. 265–276). Hershe: Information Science Publishing.

Caldwell, J. E. (2007). Clickers in the large classroom: Current research and best-practice tips. Life Sciences Education, 6 (1), 9–20.

Campt, D., and Freeman, M. (2009). Talk through the hand: Using audience response keypads to augment the facilitation of small group dialogue. The International Journal of Public Participation, 3(1), 80-107.

Campt, D., and Freeman, M. (2010) Using keypad polling to make meetings more productive, educational, and participatory. National Civic Review, Volume 99, Issue 1, pages 3–11.

Carcasson, M. and Currie, M., (2013). Click to engage: Using keypads to enhance deliberation. Center for Advancement in Public Engagement, Occasional Paper #6, 2013.

Carnaghan, C., and Webb, A. (2007). Investigating the effects of group response systems on student satisfaction, learning, and engagement in accounting education. Issues in Accounting Education, 22 (3), 391–409.

Case, S.M., and Swanson, D.B. (2002). Constructing written test questions for the basic and clinical sciences. Philadelphia: National Board of Medical Examiners.

D'Inverno, R., Davis, H., and White, S. (2003). Using a personal response system for promoting student interaction. Teaching Mathematics and Its Applications, 22(4), 163–169.

Draper, S. W., and Brown, M. I. (2004). Increasing interactivity in lectures using an electronic voting system. Journal of Computer Assisted Learning, 20(2), 81–94.

Duncan, D. (2005). Clickers in the classroom: How to enhance science teaching using classroom response systems. San Francisco: Pearson Education.

Hinde, K., and Hunt, A. (2006). Using the personal response system to enhance student learning: Some evidence from teaching economics. In D. A. Banks (Ed.), Audience response systems in higher education (pp. 140–154). Hershey: Information Science Publishing.

Horowitz, H. M. (2006). ARS evolution: Reflections and recommendations. In D. A. Banks (Ed.), Audience response systems in higher education (pp. 53–63). Hershey: Information Science Publishing.

Issacs, W. (1999). Dialogue and the art of thinking together: A pioneering approach to communicating in business and in life. Bantam Doubleday Dell Publishing Group.

Kaner, S. with Lind, L., Toldi, C., Doyle, M. (2007). Facilitator's guide to participatory decision-making. San Francisco: Jossey-Bass.

Kay, R. H., LeSage, A. (2009). Examining the benefits and challenges of using audience response systems: A review of the literature. Computers and Education 53, 819-827.

Lukensmeyer, C. (2007). Bringing Citizen Voices to the Table: A Guide for Public Managers. San Francisco: Jossey-Bass, Inc.

Rheingold, H. (2002). Smart mobs: The next social revolution. New York: Basic Books.

Schirch, L. and Campt, D., (2007). The little book of dialogue for difficult subjects: A practical hands-on guide. New York: Good Books Publishing.

Shirky, C. (2009). Here comes everybody. The power of organizing without organizations. New York: Penguin Books.

Siau, K., Sheng, H., and Nah, F. (2006). Use of classroom response system to enhance classroom interactivity. IEEE Transactions on Education, 49(3), 398–403.

Simpson, V., and Oliver, M. (2007). Electronic voting systems for lectures then and now: A comparison of research and practice. Australasian Journal of Educational Technology, 23(2), 187–208.

Slain, D., Abate, M., Hidges, B. M., Stamatakis, M. K., and Wolak, S. (2004). An interactive response system to promote active learning in the doctor of pharmacy curriculum. American Journal of Pharmaceutical Education; 68 (5) Article 117.

Surowiecki, J. (2005). The wisdom of crowds. New York: Anchor Books.

Wegerif, R. (1996). Dialogic: Education for the internet age. New York: Routledge.

Appendix 1
MAKING INTERACTIVITY WORK FOR INDIVIDUAL PRACTITIONERS

Our experience tells us that SPEIK systems are mostly reliable but are not perfectly so. Most of the time, when a breakdown occurs, the ultimate cause will later be discovered as some type of human operator error. But this is not always true. As is the case with any computer-based technology, on rare occasions, sometimes things just do not work. How do you lessen the chance of this happening? And what do you do to troubleshoot when glitches occur?

The most important thing you can do to prevent a SPEIK system from failing in front of a crowd is to go through extensive testing before the system goes live in front of the audience. We will describe the various kinds of testing that ideally we attempt to go through before every interactive polling event. We say ideally on purpose: time does not permit us to do every kind of testing for every appearance, and thankfully, the technology is reliable enough that it usually works even with only minimal testing.

For the sake of this discussion, let's assume that the polling questions have already been created. We will describe our most thorough testing regime.

CHECKLIST OF TASKS

Polling Slides, Animations, and Cross-Tabs

Some SPEIK systems have a testing mode that generates simulated polling data so that you can walk through the entire presentation. If this exists, run all of the polling questions through the simulation, asking yourself these questions:

- ☐ Do all of the polling slides work? How legible are they?
- ☐ Do the animations (such as demographic comparison data) and add-ons work? How legible are they? Do all of the transitions to and back from animations work as you expected?
- ☐ Do all of the cross-tabs work? How legible are they?
- ☐ Is there a task bar on the screen helping the facilitators manage the slides, and if so, does it obscure the content of the slide?

Input Devices

- ☐ If standalone devices are being used, do they all work on actual polling questions?
- ☐ Do you have evidence that the devices work all over the room?

Computer-to-Projector Connections

- ☐ Does the connection between the computer and the projector work?
- ☐ In some settings, there will be a need to switch a projector's input from another computer to one that will project SPEIK questions to the group. How quickly can the projector do this? How does this compare to how quickly this needs to happen so that the event flow is not disrupted?
- ☐ Have you switched from one computer to another a few times to know that it happens reliably?
- ☐ Does the SPEIK system work when connected to the on-site projector?

How The SPEIK System is Situated

- ☐ Does the physical layout of the computer and the wireless receiver remain stable on their stand?
- ☐ Does the projector fit on its stand in a way that is stable?
- ☐ Is the cord from the computer to the projector—while the machines are on their stands—long enough?
- ☐ Are all cables secured so that no one can trip over them and potentially cause the equipment to fall?

Visibility of the Graphics When Projected

☐ Does the color scheme of the results summary work well in the room when projected? This color scheme should be tested in the room, under the conditions similar to what will happen during the meeting. We have found that because of variations in projectors, as well as in natural and artificial light, the visibility of the SPEIK presentation is not something that you can determine just by looking at it on your computer.

☐ Who can you turn to during the session if a lighting or other adjustment is needed?

Workability of Audio/Video Set-Up

☐ Will there be a confidence screen for the polling facilitator other than the computer? A confidence screen is a monitor showing what is being projected to the audience so that the facilitator can see, without turning around, what the audience sees.

☐ If someone else besides the polling facilitator is advancing the polling questions, how will the presenter and the computer operator communicate if problems emerge?

☐ Will the microphone system permit the polling facilitator to be heard while ensuring the polling slides are advanced?

Day of Event

☐ Who will you call in case something goes wrong? Be sure that you have obtained all of the necessary contact information for the staff who handle issues related to the facility. These include audiovisual, internet and computer and building maintenance.

DEVICE MANAGEMENT:

- People hold onto SPEIK devices unintentionally and intentionally, so remind the group that we should all work together to make sure they all are returned.
- Lanyards can help prevent keypad disappearance by making a bigger lump in the purse, pocket, or folder.
- If you want people to wear the lanyard, create a moment where you encourage the entire group to put the lanyard on.
- Wearing the lanyard can also make people forget about the devices. Create a moment where you encourage the entire group to take the lanyard off.
- It is often useful to remind people that the devices will not open their car door, turn on their DVR, or help around their house in any way.
- To recruit people to help keep up with the keypads, it can be useful to appeal to the group and ask for their help in keeping an eye out for people leaving with the devices.
- If possible, find specific people who will be responsible for collecting a manageable number of devices (approximately five to ten). This often helps in the recounting of the devices.
- Think through how you can collect and count them in a way that is minimally disruptive to whatever is happening next.
- Making the claim that the keypads are expensive may create a greater rate of return of the devices.
- It is inevitable that someone will leave the room with a keypad in their belongings. Be sure to include your contact information on the devices so that they may be returned to you.

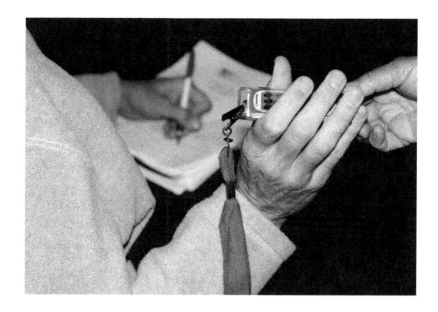

Keeping All of Your Devices

If you have sufficiently investigated these questions and answered them to your satisfaction, you are ready to hand out devices, if your SPEIK system requires that. But how will you get them back?

We have found that when trying to convey to the audience the importance of returning all of the devices, there is a communication dilemma. On the one hand, reinforcing that the devices are expensive tends to be more motivating to the participants to return the devices. On the other hand, conveying that the devices are expensive pushes participants toward thinking that polling systems are equipment for special occasions that requires the mobilization of significant resources, and not a capability that should be considered as common as microphones and projectors. You will need to decide how to thread the needle on what to communicate about this.

Playing Well With Others

If you are deploying SPEIK within an event that includes other presenters, we recommend that you adopt an "anti-diva" stance so that the other presenters or meeting organizers do not see you as an obstacle to their success. In addition, there are things that you can do outside of the presentation to provide additional value to the meeting organizer. Some specific recommendations for that are:

- If you have to deploy standalone devices, think through how you can distribute, collect, and count them in a way that does not interfere with other presentations or the overall flow of the meeting.

- If your travel logistics allow you to be at the event during other peoples' presentations, it may be to your advantage to offer to create a short polling experience to augment other speakers. Helping other presenters fine-tune their presentations by helping them read the room only adds to your perceived value in the eyes of the meeting sponsor.
- SPEIK often allows for the creation of instant reports on results. These reports can often be very useful in an on-going conference. Even if you do not take responsibility for creating a formatted report for widespread distribution, make an effort to do a quick transmittal of these reports to the meeting sponsor. It will likely be useful to remind them of the transmission text or a conversation since they may not be checking their email frequently while the meeting is taking place.

Overuse of SPEIK

Despite our love of interactivity in groups, we also know that SPEIK can be overused, for we have done this on more than one occasion. It is challenging to correctly calibrate how many times an audience can be expected to pick up their SPEIK device one more time and put their minds to that question you created in your office four days ago. If SPEIK fatigue sets in, you will see the numbers of people participating drop off, sometimes dramatically. And the feeling in the room changes. You have lost your audience, which is the greatest crime of anyone whose task it is to engage a group.

How quickly this happens is a function of many variables, such as the mood of the crowd coming in, the level of general charisma of the polling facilitator, how effectively you or someone positions SPEIK as useful to the audience's intention, the quality of the questions, how clearly they can see the polling results and hear the polling facilitator, and so on. People designing a polling experience should ask themselves hard questions: How needed is each polling inquiry? Are the questions in the right sequence? How well is this series of polling questions set up by the previous content of the gathering? How should the questions be positioned to the audience with respect to the overall flow of the agenda? Bringing a great deal of focus to these hard questions is difficult, but is much less unpleasant than being in a room where a crowd has gone from 95 percent answering questions to one where only 50 percent are answering keypad questions and the rest are talking to each other or surfing the Internet.

With all of these cautions about testing, device return, and SPEIK overuse having been said, it is important to know that in the vast majority of cases, people LOVE interactive audience polling! Rarely in our experience have they been anything but a big hit at a meeting. We are in an era in which people want to express themselves and to feel that their voices count. And people are always looking for something new. At some point, SPEIK will become something that most people have experienced; when that happens, it will be harder to please participants simply by doing an adequate job with the technology. But for at least a few more years, you can create a memorable event simply by having them work in a basic way and asking a set of questions that have a reasonable relationship to the purpose of the event.

GIVING MORE CONTROL TO THE PARTICIPANTS

One challenge that many SPEIK systems present is that you must pre-populate your answers, anticipating as best you can the range of answers your audience is likely to give. It is possible, however, to poll on open-ended questions with a little creativity. Two possibilities hold promise: using SPEIK systems with text capabilities, and having the audience generate their own list of answers for polling.

SPEIK Systems With Text Capabilities

Various SPEIK systems allow participants to text answers, which will be presented back in some visual format. The most common is the creation of a word cloud that correlates font size with word frequency. The result is a jumble of words visually representing both what each participant entered and, through size, the most commonly input ideas.

As we stated in chapter 1, we have mostly used SPEIK systems that did not have this capability. But we have used this capacity on a few occasions. For example, at an international conference on urban innovation in Spain, we arranged for the participants to get the SpotMe app on their mobile devices to answer polling questions, including open-ended questions. After one panel discussion, we asked attendees to enter one word that represented the most innovative idea they heard. The resulting word cloud showed the panelists and audience what ideas had resonated most, and allowed the facilitators to focus the large-group discussion where there was the most collective energy.

The principle drawback to this style of input is that word clouds cannot handle phrases, and treat each word separately. Thus a phrase such as "economic inequality" is parsed as two distinct entries and the phrase loses its integrity.

Audience Generated Content

Through a two-step process, you can have participants create their own answers to a question. By collecting individual answers to an open-ended question, for example through individual notes on index cards, or facilitator notes submitted manually or electronically, facilitators can sort and aggregate the input themselves. The most common submissions can be shared back with participants, who can then prioritize among the groups' own ideas instead of the facilitator's ideas generated before the meeting.

We executed this technique at a different time during the same multi-day conference mentioned earlier. For this process, scribes at table conversations took notes using the SpotMe app and submitted them in real time. Meanwhile, facilitators and conveners monitored the input from the twenty tables around the room. Table discussions were focused on challenges and opportunities in applying new learning from the conference in participants' home cities. At the end of the table discussion, table facilitators presented a list of common challenges participants face—a list which participants themselves had generated as part of a dialogue—and asked a polling question about which challenge was most relevant in the attendees' home context. Once results were displayed, a rich large group conversation ensued as participants shared frustrations and potential solutions that transcended national borders and cultures.

Although arranging such processes takes some effort, a great advantage is that people are much less likely to feel that there might be bias in the options that are voted on, since they have been created by the group.

COMPANY LISTINGS

The following is a list of companies that we believe serve the US and/or European marketplaces as of early summer 2015. We present this not as a definitive or comprehensive list, but rather as an attempt serve the reader. We apologize for any inadvertent mistakes of commission or omission.

Audience Response Rentals
http://www.audience-response-rentals.com
1-201-266-6222

Audience Response Systems, Inc.
http://www.audienceresponse.com
1-800-468-6583

Bing Pulse
http://pulse.bing.com
1-212-245-2100

ClickerSchool
http://www.clickerschool.com
1-800-338-9273

Communications Technology International Incorporated
(ComTec Audience Response Systems)
http://www.comtec-ars.com
1-201-266-6222

Double Dutch
http://doubledutch.me
1-800-748-9024

Edsurge
https://www.edsurge.com
feedback@edsurge.com

Eventpad
http://eventpad.com/contact
1-646-393-4723

iclicker
https://www1.iclicker.com
1-877-414-5922

Innovision
http://innovisioninc.com
1-800-773-7982

Inspirapps Inc.
http://polltogo.com
1-647-367-4845

Keypoint Interactive
http://www.keypointinteractive.com
1-800-773-7982

Meridia Interactive Solutions
https://www.meridiaars.com
1-610-260-6800

Option Technologies
http://optiontechnologies.com
1-888-987-8546

Padgettt Communications
http://www.pcipro.com
1-888-233-4724

Poll Everywhere*
http://www.polleverywhere.com
1-800-388-2039

Qomo Hitevision
http://qomo.com
1-248-960-985

Shakespeak
http://www.shakespeak.com
+31-0-20-716-3656
Netherlands

SmartSource Computer & Audio Visual Rentals
http://www.smartsourcerentals.com
1-800-888-8686

SMSPoll
http://www.smspoll.net
Online Contact Form

Socrative
http://www.socrative.com
Online Contact Form

Soundbite Productions Ltd.
http://soundbp.com
01962-867759
England

Top Hat Monocle Inc.
https://tophat.com
1-888-663-5491

Turning Technologies, LLC
http://www.turningtechnologies.com
1-866-746-3015

Ubiquis
http://www.ubiqus.com
1-212-346-6666

EDUCATION-SPECIFIC

81 Dash
http://81dash.com
1-866-640-6397

Answer Garden
http://answergarden.ch
Online Contact Form

Cel.ly
https://cel.ly
support@cel.ly

Classpager
https://www.classpager.com
contact@classpager.com

Engaging Technologies
http://www.engaging-technologies.com
1-800-705-4049

Geddit
http://www.letsgeddit.com
team@letsgeddit.com

Infuse Learning
http://www.infuselearning.com
Online Contact Form

iRespond
http://irespond.com
1-888-325-6565

Kahoot
https://getkahoot.com
hello@getkahoot.com

Learning Catalytics
https://learningcatalytics.com
info@learningcatalytics.com

Loca Moda
http://monstermedia.net
1-407-478-8163

Mentimeter
https://www.mentimeter.com
+46-708-65-66-09
Sweden

mQlicker
http://www.mqlicker.com
us@mqlicker.com

Padlett
http://jn.padlet.com
Online Contact Form

Plickers
https://plickers.com
1-770-855-5373

QuizSocket
http://www.quizsocket.com
http://twitter.com/svenkreiss

Renaissance Learning
http://www.renaissance.com
1-800-338-4204

The Answer Pad
http://www.theanswerpad.com
1-203-609-0271

TodaysMeet LLC
https://todaysmeet.com
help@todaysmeet.com

Verso
http://versoapp.com
1-300-762-007
Australia

---

* *Expression of Gratitude*
Because we are committed to growing the audience response field, we approached a variety of companies for assistance in helping publicize this book. We would like to specifically acknowledge Poll Everywhere for their assistance in spreading the word about this book. As the field evolves, our hope is that other companies in the industry also recognize that there can be advantages of collaborative ventures to promote audience polling.

SPEIK Features to Consider

As we have discussed, there are many capabilities that SPEIK systems can have beyond the ability of asking people to select one answer to a multiple choice question. As a service to the reader, we have put together in one place some of the characteristics we have discussed through the book. For the sake of convenience, we frame them as questions that a potential meeting organizer might ask about product offering.

Open-Ended Questions
Does the system allow for the input of text answers instead of just multiple-choice questions?

Multiple Responses
Does the system allow the creation of questions that give the participants the option of selecting more than one answer?

Anonymity

Is it possible to deploy and accept input from the SPEIK devices in a way that could give a reasonable person confidence their responses could not be easily traced back to them specifically?

Addition of External Data

Does the system allow data/images to be added to the output to help better contextualize the findings in the room?

Cross-Tabulations

Does the system allow the analysis of the way that responses to some questions may be correlated to other questions? (This might be either in real-time or post event).

Competitions

Does the system allow for participants to be easily grouped into teams and group answered compared and/or scored?

SMS Device Input

Does the system allow input through SMS messaging?

Web-Based Interface

Does the system allow input through a web-based interface, meaning that laptops, tablets, or web-enabled cell phones can serve as input devices?

Downloadable Apps

Does the systems allow input and/or display of information through apps that are downloaded to a device?

Comparing Costs

Given how widely SPEIK companies vary in not just their consumer price but their pricing structure (e.g. purchase, rental, subscription) it is very difficult to easily address the all-important question "How much would it cost to make my meetings better?" Instead of trying to provide comparison that would inevitably be accurate shortly after the publication of this book, we suggest a few parameters to think about.

While people sometimes deploy SPEIK one-time only, we advocate the SPEIK be considered a capacity that an organization or person who convenes meetings invests in with the goal of reaping the many benefits over a period of time. With that in mind, monies spent on the technology (and technical support, if applicable) are best examined with respect to cost per participant per meeting over a period of time - say two years for example. This frame allows a better comparison of costs.\

In making such a calculation, we suggest that you consider also the time costs of who ever will be designing the SPEIK questions – i.e.

serving as the meeting strategist. Unless you engage a company that positions itself as an event company, there is usually only a limited amount of assistance that SPEIK companies will provide for free in helping you customize questions to enhance meeting objectives. While ascending the learning curve for SPEIK is not extremely difficult for most meeting strategists, learning to think differently about gatherings requires some time, and this should be factored into the cost analysis. It is best if at least 2-3 people take on this task in a learning group, so they can accelerate their skills more quickly.

CPSIA information can be obtained
at www.ICGtesting.com
Printed in the USA
FSHW011249250119
55261FS